# GOING WILDE

*How I Became the Woman I Was Meant to Be by
Creating a Woman I'm Not*

## JESSICA WILDE

**ROGUE**PRESS

Published in the United States by Rogue Press.

Library of Congress Cataloging-in-Publication Data
Names: Wilde, Jessica, author.
Title: Going Wilde / Jessica Wilde
Description: Ashland, OR: Rogue Press [2021]

10 9 8 7 6 5 4 3 2 1

ISBN: 978-1-7373441-0-0
ISBN: 978-1-7373441-1-7 (eBook)

*Printed in the United States of America*

*To my beautiful daughter, Isabella.*
*You've taught me love and patience.*
*I promise to always protect you.*

*And to my darling Sophie,*
*Good girl.*

*No man, for any considerable period, can wear one face to himself and another to the multitude, without finally getting bewildered as to which may be the true.*

—Nathaniel Hawthorne

## Author's Note

I have changed the names of most people in this book. It wasn't that I didn't like their names. I just wanted to preserve their anonymity and respect their privacy. In some cases, I've also altered physical features or other particular details that might have rendered individuals easily recognizable. In a few rare instances, I've changed details of events, the description of which could put other people in jeopardy or saddle them with liability. Throughout the book, I've attempted to diligently re-create what actually happened exactly as I remember it. This is my tale, as I recall it; others may remember things differently.

# -1-

## BECOMING WILDE

I t's hard to remember all the way back to the woman I was before Jessica Wilde remade my universe in her own image. Back before boob jobs, magazine covers, full-sleeve tats, and a million Instagram followers. Before Jessica was even Jessica. Before. At one moment in time, I was nothing more than a struggling young mom who hated her life. I so badly wanted to be someone else. Actually, scratch that. The truth is that I just didn't want to be who I was. That was as far as I had gotten. I couldn't possibly have conceived of becoming a sultry social media vixen, or a magazine cover girl. My goals were much more mundane, spawned of desperation. All I wanted to achieve at that moment in time would have fit on a Post-it note. Get my ass off of public assistance for one. Find a future for my daughter, and a reasonable way out of poverty for us. That was about it. Let's be honest here; I didn't hold a lot of hope that I could achieve even one of those modest goals.

I didn't dare dream big, so there was no way I could have

known that a simple lunchtime trip to Orchard Park Shopping Centre in sleepy downtown Kelowna, British Columbia, would be the opening act to Jessica Wilde's origin story. It's just stone-cold freakish that my life would so radically and completely change courtesy of a quick visit to a bland mall in a ho-hum Canadian town.

I needed a stroller. My crappy third-hand piece of junk had given up the ghost and I was already worn out from carrying my one-year-old daughter everywhere. I'd seen an ad for a sturdy replacement on Facebook marketplace. The woman selling it was someone I knew from high school. She had never been a friend, and I hadn't even particularly liked her. She wasn't anyone I expected or wanted to see again after I dropped out in my junior year. All that was irrelevant, though. I needed that stroller.

The parking lot wasn't crowded, but I tucked my 1994 Dodge Neon into a space as far from the entrance as I could get. I hated being seen in that car. Some people say looks don't matter. They're kidding themselves. Poor people know better than anyone the harsh reality of appearances.

Poverty's like a facial burn scar—it makes the mirror your enemy, and you know everyone you meet sees it on you. People judge even if they tell themselves they don't. Being poor affects how everyone—from police, to cashiers, to Joe Average on the street—behaves toward you. You can see their thoughts written on their faces. That's not even the worst part. The most awful side to poverty is that it colors what you think of yourself. After all, you failed, right? Society teaches us that material wealth equals success. So, it follows that you must be substandard; that's the only explanation for why you're poor. Look at your bank account. You're literally worthless.

That flawed, fucked-up perspective leaves its mark on every little slice of your life. What you wear, how your hair is cut, the stroller you own and, yes, the car you drive. Want to know poverty in motion? Plant yourself in the driver's seat of a peeling-paint, barely rolling rust bucket.

I headed into the mall and made a beeline to the food court with Izzy on my hip. I had a total of twenty bucks in my pocket, money I'd taken out of our ridiculously meager household budget. I was hoping not to part with all of it because it was cash we could ill afford to spend. The mall, with all its clean, bright stores, mocked and frustrated me. I had so come to the end of my rope with being broke. At the ripe old age of twenty, I'd known money struggles as far back as I could remember. I had grown up in the red and been stuck there ever since. Now, on public assistance and heading to the food bank every Tuesday to pick up off-brand diapers, generic formula, and dented cans of soup, I felt good and truly trapped in a cage of poverty. Without consciously thinking about it, I was desperate for the key that would unlock that particular prison.

I found Sandy, the woman I would come to think of as "The Frenemy," sitting with her daughter in front of A&W. She was finishing a burger while her little girl lounged in luxury, nestled in a thickly padded faux-leather seat, inside a ride that should have had its own hood ornament. The chic black stroller had wide double wheels and beefy axles, and a frame built tough enough for off-roading. Put an engine in the thing and it would have been nicer than my Neon. The one she was selling sat next to the table, set up and ready to roll. It might have paled in comparison to her daughter's ride, but it was a hundred times better than what my broken stroller had ever been.

She jumped up to greet me, gave me a barely-touching hug and an air kiss, and made a big show of how good I looked. I knew that trick. It was her way of emphasizing how much better she looked than I did. She didn't even have to play that game. The woman was decked out in ten kinds of style.

There I was in my well-worn black leggings and beat-up black hoodie, looking like some sort of female burglar wannabe. And there she was in brand-new True Religion jeans and baby blue lululemon sweater, with a Louis Vuitton handbag swinging from her shoulder. She might not have been the most beautiful woman in the world—a tall and stocky blonde built more like a field hockey fullback than a runway walker, with a pinched face and close-set eyes—but that didn't matter. Drape any woman in the right fitting designer labels and a ton of swag and she's bound to look good. I could literally feel how odd a couple we made standing there.

"Why don't we take a loop around the mall? You can try out the stroller and it'll give us a chance to catch up."

It worked for me, because I had no money to spend on a food court lunch or even a soda. I wasn't exactly thrilled at the idea of spending the afternoon with her, but I didn't have anywhere else to be. I buckled Izzy into the stroller and we headed off in the general direction of the cineplex. I tried to ignore the obvious pleasure she was taking in our different circumstances. More than anything, though, I was puzzled at how exactly she could afford all that bling. She was a single mom. I knew her parents didn't have any money. I pried as best I could but she wasn't giving anything away. Instead, she made small talk about people we knew from high school.

We stopped at almost every clothing store along the way. Something sparkly would grab her eye and she would run inside, only to come out a few minutes later with another bag. I waited outside each time. All the shopping only made me more curious. She seemed to have an unlimited bankroll. It also started to make sense why she wanted to meet there. Grab lunch, sell a stroller, and get in some quality shopping all in one stroke. Halfway around the mall, a gaggle of fancy bags hung from the handles of her daughter's stroller. I had seen enough and was tired of being reminded of all the stuff I couldn't hope to buy. I told her I had to get going.

"Okay, well it was great seeing you."

"Yeah, you too."

There was a pregnant pause as she waited for something. Finally, her smile faded a little. "You want the stroller?"

I had completely forgotten about the stroller. "Oh, yeah, of course." Izzy had fallen asleep and I pulled a stuffed animal out from underneath her. "Is there any chance you'd take less than twenty?" I knew the answer before the words were out of my mouth.

She pursed her lips as if she were really considering it. "I don't think so. It's in perfect condition." She flashed a fake sympathetic smile.

"Alright, no problem." I pulled the crumpled twenty out of my pocket and reluctantly handed it to her. "I'll see you around."

"I'll walk out with you."

Her brand-new midnight-blue BMW was parked three spots from the door. We said our goodbyes with another Hollywood hug and air kiss, and I hustled away from her like I actually had some place to be.

As I drove home, I couldn't stop thinking about The Frenemy's bling. Designer clothes, haute couture purse, lux stroller. Where did all that come from? I couldn't let it go. I mulled over the puzzle. The mental picture of the two of us side by side hurt me somewhere deep down inside my soul.

As much as she wanted to lord her money over me or pretend she was better than I was, we came from the similar humble circumstances. We had been raised in the same lower middle-class world, and had both given birth when we were still teenagers. Then something changed. Something big. What was her secret? That entire walk through the mall, she never mentioned a job and we had met in the middle of a weekday. I knew her baby daddy and he wasn't the make-it-big type. If it was a well-heeled boyfriend, she would surely have taken the chance to brag. So how in the heck was she able to afford all that stuff? Two-hundred-dollar jeans and a brand-new Beamer?

I could not get that question out of my head, even hours after I got home. It was an itch I couldn't scratch. Finally, curiosity got the best of me and I messaged her on Facebook, bluntly asking,

"How do you afford everything?"

About a twenty minutes later, the phone rang. It was her. "I'm going to tell you something and you can't tell anyone. This is just between you and me." I got the distinct feeling that she hated letting me in on her secret, but hated missing the chance to brag even worse.

"Yeah, of course." What could it be? Mary Kay cosmetics? Drug dealing? Robbing banks?

"You have to promise."

"I promise."

Finally, after a long pause, she said, "I'm a cam girl."

I knew about camming. Guys went online and paid girls in video chat rooms to do sexual stuff on camera. Some cam girls set up cameras in every room of their house and guys paid to watch them take showers or even sleep. Mostly, though, the camera was set up in the bedroom and the guys made sex requests. "Wait, what? You make all that money just by camming?"

"I make a ton of money. You know, you could too."

I had lost sixty pounds after my daughter was born, but I wasn't confident that anyone would pay to see me naked. I had stretch marks and saggy boobs. Even though I was my own worst critic, you didn't need a critical eye to see that I looked a little rode hard for a twenty-year-old. Still, a "ton of money" sounded like an amount I could get used to.

"How would I even get started?"

"Sign up on the service I use. They take a cut. They process all the money and handle the web stuff. They take care of everything. All you need is a computer, a good webcam, and a dildo."

"It's that easy?"

"Well, there's everything you have to do on camera. It's work. You'd be surprised at what guys are like. The host collects all the money and wires you your payment every two weeks, right into your bank account." I heard ice clinking in her glass on the other end of the line.

"How much can you make?"

She laughed. "I pulled in four thousand last month. A couple hours a day." I held back a gasp. Given what little my husband and I made, that kind of coin would be a complete and utter game changer. She told me she would give me pointers if I decided to do it, and we agreed to talk soon. I hung up and sat looking at the phone for a minute. "I'll be damned," I thought. "That bitch just gave me the golden ticket."

There was no question I would do it. It wasn't a moral issue for me. Here's the thing about morals—they're a luxury. There's a reason they call it "crushing poverty"; it grinds you down into dust. Living in poverty, you learn that "fair" doesn't determine who has money and who doesn't.

Like a lot of poor people, I had an unwarranted sense that I was meant for something more than the average bear. When you struggle to survive, just to eat and keep a roof over your head, you don't spend a lot of time pondering the nuances of good and evil. Everything about your life chafes you and there's one answer for it all: money. At that moment in time, I was driven by one thought: "I don't want to be poor anymore."

It meant going into overdraft in our bank account, but it was a risk I was willing to take because camming looked like my Hail

Mary escape out of a life that I hated. I headed upstairs and told my husband, Bobby, about my plan. He was understandably not thrilled.

"No way. I don't want you to do that."

"Too bad. I'm doing it."

We both knew the sad truth; he had no juice to stop me. I had always held the upper hand in our relationship because he was devoted to me and I had never felt the same way.

"Please, don't."

"What are we going to do? This is our only chance."

He slumped forward and hung his head. It was as if a part of him had dissolved and what was left couldn't hold its own weight up. It wasn't just jealousy. I'm sure there was a part of him that knew full well I was not only on my way out of the marriage, but that I was already gone. Financial independence was going to mean total independence, including from him. Any success, any new stream of income, was just going to speed up the inevitable.

Bobby was the type of person who made the most of whatever hand he had been dealt. He had no driving ambitions beyond his dedication to Izzy and me. As long as he had us and his love for us, he was willing to work any shitty job making a miserable paycheck. He didn't ask for much out of life; his grandest aspiration at that point amounted to slowly saving up money for the next generation Xbox.

In a way, I envied him. He rolled with the punches and wasn't constantly bothered by poverty the way I was. He felt that you did what you could in life, but when you were up against something you couldn't change, you made your peace with it. His perspective was one of the many ways we differed. Those differences wrote the conclusion of our relationship long before we lived it. From the start, we had just been two damaged, wounded kids clinging to each other. That was never the same as a relationship.

If I hadn't thought there was so much on the line and been so focused on escape, I might have mustered more compassion. Maybe I would have even felt bad for Bobby and tried to reassure him somehow. He was a wonderful guy and losing someone who you know deep down you never really had, has to be an emotional hell. I didn't treat him well for most of our relationship, and I didn't give him any say in the matter when it came to camming. Although I would not openly admit it to myself, I unreasonably felt that he was part of the problem. I put it on him that he was just another sign of poverty in my unwanted life, the human equivalent of a 1994 Dodge Neon.

The next morning, I marched through the glass doors of the bank five minutes after the place opened. I took out an overdraft for a hundred dollars. We now had exactly negative one hundred dollars in our account. Once you're at zero, though, what does it matter? I felt like there really wasn't a whole lot left to lose and it seemed like a smart gamble from where I stood. The next stop was Staples, where I picked out the best webcam I could afford. That was the easy purchase. Buying a dildo was a bit more brutal.

I had never been inside a sex shop. I picked a little store downtown that was run by a middle-aged woman. For whatever reason, I thought that would make me feel more comfortable. It didn't. The experience was nerve-racking. I was self-conscious and unreasonably worried about being judged the moment I reluctantly stepped through the blacked-out glass door.

It was a bit of crazy thinking on my part; the other people in the store weren't there for bible study, and they weren't about to look down their noses at me. Standing just inside the door, bracing myself to go deeper into the maze of raunchy videos and exotic contraptions and sex toys, the seriousness of what I was about to do hit me. There is only one reason you buy a dildo for camming. I could suddenly visualize what the experience was going to be like, and I began to have a hard time breathing.

As awful as that mental picture was, there were actually darker thoughts bouncing around inside my head. For the first time since I started the ball rolling on what could be this new profession, I realized that there was a possibility no guy would pay to see me nude. It was a sobering thought, but the more I considered it, the more realistic it seemed. What if I was all alone on that cam feed with a blank chat screen? What if I turned off the computer after an hour having made absolutely no money— having actually blown a hundred bucks for nothing? What then? I worked myself up into a nice little panic attack. "If this doesn't work," I thought, "I'm really fucking up with our rent money right now. I could put us out on the street."

I couldn't shake that anxiety as I tentatively made my way through the shop, the fluorescent fixtures flickering overhead. I fought the entirely reasonable urge to cut and run. Finally, I found the dildos displayed on a rack behind the counter. I picked out the most realistic and average-sized one they had. I assumed no guy would want to see a fake dick that would put his own to shame. It also seemed logical that the more realistic a dildo was, the more relatable it would be to the person on the other side of the camera. Still, as the cashier rang up my purchase, I had an overwhelming urge to tell her that I was buying it for business, not because I was some horny chick. As if she would have cared.

I had never been so happy to slide into the safe haven of my Neon's driver seat, the dildo safely hidden in a white plastic bag. I sat there willing myself to breathe slow and steady. There were going to be harder hills to climb in this crazy plan of mine.

The closer I got to what I was actually about to do, the more real it became and the more nervous I got. I felt like I had started a huge boulder rolling. I had committed and now there was no turning back. I had the feeling of watching myself do something rather than experiencing it in the first person. I took a deep breath.

At the very least, it felt good to take control for a change. Life had for so long happened to me one gut punch at a time. Like I was riding along in a fast-moving river, through rapids. To that point in my life, it was all I could do to keep my head above the surface. Now, though, I had a chance to get out of the water. "You want this," I kept thinking, "It's the answer. It's going to change everything." I had a hard time believing myself.

When I got home, I ignored Bobby and headed upstairs to our ancient desktop computer. Setting up the webcam was easy because it was essentially plug-and-play. When I was done, I pushed my chair back from the computer monitor that now had this black, unblinking eye attached to the top of it. I looked at the camera lens. It had some sort of incredible power, this simple little electronic gizmo that could transform my life. It would capture the unspeakable and could be a pipeline to money. Problem was, I couldn't possibly understand all the ways it was going to change who I was. I had no idea who Jessica Wilde was, what she held in store for my life, and how she would challenge me. I didn't fully grasp that even the most positive life changes have unintended consequences. That was a lesson I would eventually learn the hard way.

I went online and found the cam host site. Setting up my account was easy, but I stumbled when it came to picking a screen name. The cursor blinked steadily on and off. The Frenemy had stressed that the first rule of camming was to create an identity to hide behind. It wouldn't do to have neighbors or some distant relative popping onto the site and finding my page. I knew that bad things could happen if the wrong "client" figured out who I was in real life.

Spies call them "covers." Undercover federal agents call them "legends." For a cam girl, an alternate identity starts with a screen name. I typed in "Tat Goddess," because I already had almost a half sleeve of tattoos on one arm and a butterfly tramp stamp covering my lower back. I picked out a random clip art illustration of a big-breasted zombie woman for my avatar photo. It was eye-catching and didn't reveal anything about me.

The Frenemy had told me that I also needed a real-world name on my account, one that guys could call me in the course of a normal conversation. It had to be something more standard and relatable than my screen name. My best friend when I was growing up had been a beautiful girl named Jessica. She had the olive skin, ebony eyes, and long, thick brown hair of her Italian heritage. I had always loved her name and associated it with what I thought were her exotic looks. She and I had stayed tight right through high school and beyond, forming a group with other girls who were also on the outside looking in. Each of us dropped out and got pregnant. It was a good support network during a time in my life when I was completely lost.

Unfortunately, shortly after I gave birth to Izzy and began to lose weight while Jessica continued to gain it, she decided out of the blue that I was sleeping with her husband. It was a delusional, completely fabricated accusation. That didn't stop her from being absolutely certain that it was true and out for blood. She trashed me to the others in our little support group. One by one, all the girls wrote me off. My social network shrunk to zero.

I'm not sure exactly why I chose her name. Maybe there was a tiny part of me that felt it was a form of revenge. Maybe I just wanted to turn that sad memory into something more positive. Whatever the reason, I became "Jessica." People had told me for years that I looked like the actress Olivia Wilde. So, bingo. I had my last name. Jessica Wilde, a woman Frankensteined into existence to make money. If only I had known then all that she would become, that one day my monster creation would attempt to gobble up the real me … well, I would probably have created her anyway.

I finished setting up my account by blocking most of Canada and anywhere in the United States that I had family. Following The Frenemy's lead, I decided to log on for the first time that afternoon, after Izzy went down for her nap. She was sound asleep when I crept into the bedroom I shared with Bobby, just after three in the afternoon. I moved the bed within range of the camera and went live as Jessica Wilde for the first time. I was more nervous than I had ever been in my life.

I struggled with the rising panic as I felt every muscle in my body tense up. My avatar was marked with a "new" tag, which drew guys to check me out. They started typing comments in my window, and the panel quickly filled with text. I was so stressed out that I couldn't speak. It had seemed like such a basic interaction: someone I couldn't see typed something in a chat window and then I was supposed to verbally reply on camera. One of the "clients" could ask me to go private, where he'd pay by the minute for me to do whatever he wanted to watch. Experienced cam girls drew that process out, racking up money on the "meter." Clients could also tip. Starting out, though, I was simply overwhelmed. That basic back-and-forth seemed horribly complicated and way beyond my abilities. I had to fight the urge to run for the door.

It took me almost thirty minutes before I could actually talk back to anyone on the other side of the camera. I was surprised to find the guys in my public chat encouraging and helpful. They were rooting for me. I even naively asked what I should charge for different requests, like taking my top off. They were amazingly supportive.

When it came time to get naked, I was absurdly self-conscious. I was already insecure about my body and the toll my daughter's birth, and rapid weight loss after, had taken. Even worse, it felt like a violation. I had experienced a lot of sexual abuse, and even rape, in my life. The cam experience seemed hauntingly familiar. I could hear Bobby moving around in the kitchen, but he seemed a million miles away. I knew rationally I had control. I could easily switch off the computer if I wanted. Just as real, though, was the sense that I was surrendering control and being forced into something. It was so confusing. I tried not to let my thoughts run away with me, to trick my mind into believing this was any different than making sandwiches at Subway. It was just a job I was doing, something I would get through and then could go live my "real" life. I absolutely had to get my head right if I was going make camming work. There was simply no way around baring my body for complete strangers.

Ultimately, the fact that I couldn't see anyone else was the saving grace. In a way, the sheer absurdity of me taking my clothes off and masturbating in front of a tiny electronic eyeball made it easier to push forward. It was different, I realized, than someone laying their hands on me against my will. The guy on the other side of that eyeball? Well, out of sight, out of mind. Mostly I could fool myself into believing it was just me and my computer having a fun old time with a store-bought dildo.

Still, it was constantly confusing. A little voice deep inside my head kept saying, "You know you're better than this, and your body is sacred, and these people don't really deserve to see you naked for any amount of money." The louder voice, though, was screaming, "You're providing for your family. This is the way out. You're not hurting anyone. No one is really physically hurting you. How can it be abuse if no one is touching you?" On and on it went. I tried my best not to think at all, just act.

I logged off two hours later, completely exhausted. I checked my account and couldn't believe my eyes. Staring at the daily balance, I thought, "Holy shit, I just made two hundred bucks in two hours." It had been brutal, but if that money was the true measure of what I could do every day, there was a clear, bright light at the end of the tunnel. Izzy and I were on our way toward a better life, a place where I wouldn't be constantly worried about money. Camming was the answer I had been searching for.

I played a sort of mental game with the physical reality of camming. I didn't have to go through the actual work on camera. I had created Jessica Wilde for that, and she had just made me two hundred dollars. She did the hard stuff; I enjoyed the money. It dawned on me that she had earned all that money with what I knew to be her imperfections. Her thin lips and saggy boobs. Her thighs that I had never really liked. I had to wonder what she might earn if she was everything she could be. If I made her better. You could literally be anybody online. I could make Jessica Wilde whoever I wanted—or needed—her to be.

People think that they are covering up the blemishes when they paint a better life on Facebook or Instagram. They are actually doing what I had done that day—becoming someone they are not. It was reassuring to know I wasn't alone. Some housewife in Manitoba or Michigan, with her cheesy photoshopped photos of the lake vacation and close-ups of holiday sugar cookies she had to ice three times to get just right for the camera? She was creating her own Jessica Wilde. I was just going further with it. She did it for adoration, to rack up likes. I did it for cold, hard cash. That was my second big epiphany—you could make a bundle being exactly the right person online.

I went upstairs to hug Izzy and let Bobby know that I was done. At least for that day. Looking at Bobby's profoundly sad face, I didn't have the heart to tell him about the money or what I had just done in our bedroom. I had never seen him so obviously depressed and I felt guilty. Not guilty enough to quit, though. I was still high from having made more in two hours than I would have earned in a week putting together sandwiches at Subway, handling the register at a car wash, or cleaning hotel rooms. Like me, Bobby was just going to have to get used to our new reality. Jessica Wilde was now Queen Bitch in our house. She was here to help and she would do what she needed to do to earn us a better life. But we all needed to wrap our heads around the fact that she was here to stay.

# -2-

# A Little Wilde

My identity was confused from the moment I was born. My mother was only sixteen when she gave birth to me in an unwed mothers home. Two weeks later, she surrendered me for adoption. The adoption agreement specified that my new parents had to keep the name she had given me—Samantha. The woman who would be the only mother I would ever really know changed my name to Tiffany. Jessica Wilde would be my third identity. Who lives in your mirror? I see three faces looking back—the girl I could have been, the woman I am, and the woman I created. They often blur together.

My biological mother had also insisted that she be allowed to visit me. My adopted parents never honored that part of the agreement either. In fact, the first and last time I ever laid eyes on my birth mother was at her funeral. I had just turned five when my parents told me and my brother to dress in our best clothes so they could take us to the chapel. We were regularly dragged along to church on Sunday, but it wasn't Sunday. I had never seen a funeral, and had no real understanding of what "dead" meant. My adopted parents told me up front who the woman in the casket was. Even still, I struggled to wrap my tiny head around how that young, pretty woman in the casket was related to me. How do you process losing something you never knew you had?

Death, loss, surprise reveal. All of those would have been plenty to keep my young mind spinning, but there was more. An infant girl was nestled in beside my birth mother. My half sister. The mortician had done a good job. Mother and baby looked serene and as natural as a twenty-year-old and infant could look laid out in a satin-lined, lacquered brown box. To me, they didn't appear upset or worried; they looked peaceful and kind of happy.

I was fascinated with my birth mother. She had a simple, attractive face with features that were still girlish. Her long, shiny brown hair had been carefully arranged to frame her face. I thought that she looked like a nice person. The baby was just a baby, like any baby. I could not find any feeling inside me that connected me to her. I asked my adopted mother if I could touch the woman in the casket. She looked over at an attendant who nodded ever so slightly. I reached in and laid my hand on my mother's rouged cheek. I was shocked to find her skin was almost ice cold to the touch.

There was another coffin, too. It held the body of my mother's boyfriend. The three of them had been killed in a car accident. I was uncomfortable with all the long faces lining the pews, and doe-eyed pitying looks people gave me. I didn't like the attention. Everything seemed strange and far away. My memories of that day are faded snapshots now: the coldness of a dead woman's skin, the fake look of the heavy makeup against the stark white of blood-drained cheeks. The muted sound of someone crying softly. Long rectangles of jewel-colored light cast across the carpet by the sun shining through the stained glass windows. Those are the memories of my biological mother—a few random images and a lot of unanswered questions that I wasn't mature enough at the time to even form, much less ask.

It was a surreal day in an otherwise happy, mundane, and typical middle-class suburban existence. My adopted mother had learned she was pregnant after she and her husband had already started the ball rolling on my adoption. I wound up with a brother only a few months younger than I was. We were playmates growing up, spending hours together running around with abandon in our overgrown backyard. The blue-and-white three-bedroom ranch house on Rundlemere Court was right out of a Home Depot ad. There was a white picket fence out front and we each had our own bedroom. Life would have been a pile of puppies if nothing had ever changed.

Things do change, though, often traumatically. I was sexually abused for the first time that same year. For some reason, my parents hired a thirty-something guy who lived down the street to babysit my brother and me when they went out. The babysitter was a short, unattractive man with a painfully phony smile and a creepy way of talking to children. He smelled of Irish Spring soap and made my skin crawl.

After he put my brother to bed, he kept me in the living room and I pretended to fall asleep because he made me nervous. He picked me up and laid me on top of him and began rubbing my body along his. I kept my eyes shut tight, hoping that he would stop and leave me alone. When my parents finally came home and walked in, he pretended to be asleep. As if we had simply fallen asleep one on top of the other. I was confused that they couldn't see the situation for what it was. Like most children, I thought my parents should have been all-seeing, all-knowing. I had no idea what I was supposed to do to stop him, only that I didn't want this man touching me. That didn't seem to matter to the adults in the house. I had no language to voice protest, and it felt as if I had no way to protect myself.

My parents had always fought, but the arguments got worse and worse. Eventually, shouting became the soundtrack of our house. A few months after my birth mother's funeral, the battle came to a head and my parents split up. That marked the start of a long, slow downward spiral for my mother, brother, and me. It would be the last time I would feel safe, wanted, accepted, and truly part of a family. The search to recapture those things would turn my life upside down from then on, as it does to some degree even now.

My brother and I were given the cruelest of choices: mom or dad. Even at five, I knew that we were being set up to lose no matter what we decided. When we were with one or the other, my parents tore each other down. It was ugly, but someone had to be lying. Ultimately, my brother and I made the wrong choice. We chose to stay with my mother. My father headed off to greener pastures and turned the page with a young divorcee and her two children.

My mom, on the other hand, struggled to find happiness and

stability. It could not have been easy to be a suddenly single mother with two small children. We pinballed around as she struggled through a series of low-paying jobs and boyfriend after boyfriend. She eventually trained and started working as a licensed practical nurse at a nursing home.

Men came and went in our lives. The common threads were that they all had more money than we did, and were rarely in our lives for long. Even when my brother and I found ourselves living in a tidy, well-tended ranch house along a tree-lined street, we knew better than to get comfortable. The fighting would start, things would be said that couldn't be taken back or soothed over, and the bags would get packed.

Onto the next place, next guy, next situation. The men got progressively older as the homes became smaller and smaller. We found ourselves in dicier neighborhoods as our little family unit became ever more dysfunctional.

I can't imagine it was unusual that my mother seemed to favor my brother over me. After all, he was her flesh and blood. At night, she would cuddle with him on one end of the couch while I sat alone on the other end. I don't think she did it to spite me; she simply wasn't aware of a disparity that was all too painfully clear to me. If there was one slice of Sara Lee cake left, one Twist & Shout cookie in the package, we all knew who got it. The second-class status left me feeling increasingly abandoned, unloved, and alienated. Those feelings would become all too familiar. Day to day, it seemed as if I didn't really belong anywhere and wasn't worth much.

Where could I turn? I didn't have a father, or an older brother.

There was no uncle or wise aunt who would reassure me. I was keenly aware, from the age of six on, that I had no real place in a family. I wasn't "family" to anyone. It was a lesson, a harsh realization. I understood that I had to compartmentalize fear and sadness. There was not going to be any protection from the bad in the world. I was exposed and vulnerable.

At that young age, alone in my bed and sad to my core, I learned to take refuge in a nameless detached numbness. Sexual abuse, abandonment, neglect. All those things happened to someone else named Tiffany. I was numb, and separate from all that. The numbness would become my reliable defense, a hiding place from the world's terrors. If I couldn't stop bad things from happening, I could retreat behind a blank, white-noise wall, a place outside feeling and thinking. It would be my only relief from the incidents of abuse and trauma that were to come.

A year later, a teenage boy who lived across the street cornered me behind some bushes and exposed himself. He forced me to touch his genitals. I was repulsed and scared. I broke away and ran home to tell my mother. She made light of it. "Oh, you children out there playing doctor." Perhaps she honestly thought I was exaggerating about what had happened.

She was trying to manage two children, run a house, and hold down a job. There may have been denial involved, a refusal to register what could be a serious problem and huge neighborhood blow-up. I was, though, completely perplexed and disappointed. Wasn't I supposed to turn to adults, to trust them to keep me safe?

Didn't bad behavior get punished? Didn't all the things we had learned since preschool—that you keep your hands to your own body, stranger danger and all that—mean anything? Was it all just so much nonsense?

Those early experiences not only instilled in me a general mistrust of people, a wariness that would mark me for the rest of my life, it also created a sexual confusion that would loom large in my emotional development. I had no substantive role model in my life, no authoritative source of guidance about what constituted safe or healthy sex. My mother, like so many others, simply wasn't equipped to sit me down and educate me in that way. No one would ever teach me what the borders were, much less how to set rules and what to do when they were broken. I wrestled with an overwhelming sense of powerlessness. There was nothing I could do about anything. I hated that feeling.

I think my mother was overwhelmed with life at that point. There was virtually no parental supervision in my youth. Lacking direction, I made horrible decisions. One of the worst was getting drunk for the first time when I was nine. I had gone to stay with my father and his new family, which meant sharing a bedroom with my stepsister Danielle. She was six years older and the popular girl I so badly wanted to be. I envied her. She had a large circle of friends and an important, secure place within my father's new family. She was wanted, loved, and confident. I craved the life she had and badly ached to fit into that family if I could. I desperately wanted to find my *place*.

Danielle was understandably less than thrilled to have a nine-year-old girl she barely knew sharing her room. She was even less thrilled that my father and stepmother saddled her with babysitting me while they went out for the night. Danielle had big plans and I was a fly in the ointment. Four of her girlfriends were coming over for a night of drinking, and she couldn't have me spilling the beans. In her mind, that meant I had to be involved, as guilty as the rest.

"Look, don't embarrass me when my friends get here. We're all going to be drinking, so you have to drink, too."

"I don't think I should." I was nine. I liked staying at my father's house. I loved the mid-century décor and how stylish the house seemed to me. I wanted to be welcomed as one of them. I wanted to follow the rules and make my father and stepmother happy. I didn't want to rock the boat.

Of course, I also wanted to fit in with Danielle's group, with the cool ones. I was faced with a paradox. I wanted to keep Danielle happy, but drinking booze was a shockingly serious violation of the rules. I was also scared of what alcohol would do to me. I'd seen my share of drunk adults acting like idiots. I didn't fancy the idea of being a clown in front of people I envied and wanted to impress.

You like having fun, don't you?"

"Yeah, sure."

"Well then ... drinking is fun. You're going to like it."

I twisted a strand of my hair and focused on the shag carpet. The last thing I wanted was to disappoint Danielle or make her mad. I was profoundly conflicted, though. I seemed like such a dangerous line to cross. "Is it going to make me act weird? I don't want to do anything stupid."

"It just makes you feel really good."

"But I won't, like, lose control of my body or anything?"

"What? No. I'll be here. You want to be cool, right? Everyone will think you're cool. That's all."

She had found exactly the right button to push. Cool. Yep, I so very much wanted to be as cool as the North Pole. I wanted these chicks to spread the word that "cool" was my middle name. The idea of being cool captured everything I was after—friends who thought I was worth hanging out with, a group that accepted me, liked me, and had my back. I wanted family, but if all I could hope for was a gang of older girls letting me into their inner circle, I would gladly take it.

"Okay."

Danielle filled a highball glass with a half-and-half mix of orange juice and vodka. She stirred it with a butter knife and handed me the glass. It looked innocent enough. I took a sip. It tasted chemical, more biting than plain OJ. The second sip was easier. Ten minutes later, I had drained the glass. I was almost instantaneously drunk.

Danielle and her friends thought it was hilarious, this nine-year-old stumbling around the room slurring her words and talking nonsense. It must have been entertaining ... right up to the moment I started vomiting everywhere. Danielle got a rough dose of karma that night. She had to wrap the party early so that she could clean up puke and get me into bed before her parents walked through the door.

Danielle was the devil on my shoulder. Like any young teen, she took the path of least resistance and dragged me along into her misadventures rather than have me ruin the good times. Not only did she pour me my first drink, she taught me how to smoke. At eleven, my mom sent me off to spend a month with my father's family over summer break. A week after I got there, I walked in on Danielle sharing a cigarette with two of her girlfriends. She panicked. We both knew I was supposed to make a beeline for my dad and tell on everyone. Smoking was bad. It caused cancer. Danielle was having none of it. Wouldn't it be so much better if I just joined in and got a premium pass to that ever-elusive "cool"? Didn't I want to be like her and her friends? Part of the gang?

Oh, you betcha I did.

She taught me how to inhale smoothly and exhale without hacking. I felt sick that first time, but quickly became a seasoned smoker. It's a terrible skill for an eleven-year-old to have, but lighting up and taking a deep hit felt like the coolest I'd ever been. Maybe I wasn't as popular as Danielle, but I now had a place inside the inner circle. I was allowed to tag along on trips to meet her friends at the mall, where I would be a human party trick.

Danielle would say, "Hey, wanna see a little kid smoke?"

She'd tap out a cigarette from her pack of Du Mauriers and I would light it up as if it were something I did every day. Which, already, was the case. I had become a pack-a-day smoker within that first month. It felt natural. I basked in it; I *belonged* there, outside the glass doors of the mall, with a half dozen other kids.

My new habit fit right in back home. After another relationship went bad, my mom had moved us into a beat-up single-wide in the ironically named Paradise Mobile Home Park. It was a desperate place full of desperate people. Danielle had been a bad influence because I was so impressionable, but she was a Girl Scout compared to some of the friends I made in that trailer park.

Paradise was a white-trash stronghold. Nobody planned for the future or weighed the consequences of what they did. For most of us, there would be no future to speak of. It was a hopeless place where kids ran loose, untethered by commonsense rules. None of us did homework. Few really expected to make it all the way through high school, much less on to college, so what was the point?

Sex was a part of the desperation. I had my first period the year we moved there. I developed a crush on a seventeen-year-old boy who lived in the park with his mom. He was tall and skinny, with the longest eyelashes I had ever seen on a boy. One afternoon, as we sprawled in the living room of a friend's trailer watching TV, he started kissing me. It was exciting. He whispered in my ear, "I'm going to be your first." At eleven, having never had any instruction or guidance that could qualify as "sex education," I didn't understand what he meant. I knew for certain, though, that I would gladly do whatever he wanted if he would love me.

He led me into the bathroom and forced me down onto the cold vinyl floor. He pulled my jeans and underpants off and tossed them aside. I felt the numbness, my natural defense, wash over me. Something was wrong about all this. He shouldn't be doing what he was doing, but I felt powerless to stop it. It wasn't at all how I had envisioned our love affair unfolding.

I once again had the sense of watching things happen from

outside my body. It seemed like only a split second before he was on top of me, and then inside me. It hurt, but the numbness kept the pain separate. The tiny room seemed to fill with the smell of him, and I took short, shallow breaths to avoid it. I turned my head to the side and saw the bloody pad in my underwear, my clothes bunched up against the edge of the flesh-colored tub. It was an ugly moment in a horrible place. He made the noises men make and, as quickly as it had started, it was over. He stood up, tucked himself in, and zipped up. He looked embarrassed and seemed on the verge of saying something. After an uncomfortable moment of silence, he simply turned and walked out. I got dressed, still numb. There was a buzzing in my head. It hadn't worked; I didn't feel loved or accepted. Instead, I felt the exact opposite—used and discarded. I got myself together and quickly headed home.

My mother found me in the bathroom, just sitting on the vanity lost in thought. She could sense that something was off. "What happened?"

I told her in detail. Hindsight is risky business and it's a mistake to judge another parent by way of a rearview mirror. I can tell you this, though, as a mother. If my eleven-year-old daughter had told me what I told my mom that day, I would have gone scorched earth on that young man. My mom? I'm sure she did what she thought was best for me. That meant popping me into the car, driving me down to the walk-in clinic and, before I could really process what was happening, getting me set up with a prescription for birth control pills.

On the drive home, I stared out the window. I wondered if

there was a magic age when things would get better. I didn't hate my mother but I couldn't honestly say I loved her, either. She was just the person in charge right now and she was doing a pretty shit job of it as far as I was concerned. I knew, even if I couldn't have put it into words, that I was on my own. I had to look out for myself as best I could.

Unfortunately, I wasn't particularly good at doing that. Like most of the kids in the trailer park, I drank almost every day. There was little else to do and there was a lot of alcohol around. On Canada Day, my friends and I went "cooler hopping," roaming through the campsites of holiday partiers along Okanagan Lake, stealing cans of Molson as we went. We all ended up tremendously drunk. I fell asleep on the floor of a friend's bedroom. I woke up late the next morning, knowing I was in big trouble. My mother was furious when I walked through the door, hungover and apologetic.

"Where the hell were you?"

"I'm sorry. I fell asleep at Abby's house."

"You couldn't bother to call? I was worried sick."

"I'm sorry."

I felt way too bad to even mount a decent defense. I couldn't think straight for the headache and dry mouth. She stared at me but I had nothing. The frustration was written on her face; her life was a struggle and I was adding exponentially to that hardship. "You know what? I've had enough of your bullshit. I'm not going to deal with it anymore. Pack your stuff because you're going to live with your dad. You can be his problem from now on."

A day to circle on the calendar: the first time my mother

kicked me out. It was just one more in a series of rejections. It was like the universe was screaming, "You're not wanted." It's a terrible feeling for an eleven-year-old to experience. As punishments go, moving to my father's wasn't much. I didn't feel welcome in either place, so it didn't matter where I laid my head. My mom bought me a ticket on the Greyhound bus for the next day, and I headed off on the twelve-hour ride to my father's house in Calgary.

I was the unwelcome houseguest from the moment I stepped through the door. I felt so out of place that I didn't even dare go into the kitchen and get a glass of water or make myself something to eat. I was posted in Danielle's room once again and she let me know that somehow, in my absence, I had been evicted from the inner circle. I was no longer cool and she wanted nothing to do with me.

My strategy was to steer clear of everyone as much as possible. We ate dinner together every night. That was my favorite time because it gave me the chance to indulge the fantasy of being part of a family. The rest of the time, though, I hunkered down on my bed with my stepbrother Mark's Discman clamped over my ears while the rest of the family watched TV. I was there, but I did my best to disappear.

My father enrolled me in a middle school a few blocks from the house, but I did no better in my classes than I had ever done. I was so far behind, so lost in the coursework, that the teachers might as well have been speaking Greek. My father and stepmother never checked my homework. I suspect they didn't want to deal with the challenge that would face them if they did. They also let me smoke outside because I was hooked and would do it anyway.

To his credit, my father made an effort to straighten me out. He signed me up for a youth basketball league and even came to my weekly games. Unfortunately, it wasn't enough to give me a sense of place or purpose. I was a poor athlete, which didn't endear me to my teammates. Instead, I looked for acceptance and belonging among my middle-school classmates, hoping to become the popular girl at my school that I imagined Danielle was at the high school.

One day at lunch break, I convinced a group of girls that we should head to my house and dip into my father's liquor stash. I wanted to impress those kids and assumed we could have a few drinks and then slip back into school with no one the wiser. It was a flawed calculation.

These weren't friends from the trailer park, kids with built-up tolerances and the understanding of how to pace themselves and maintain their composure in the presence of authority figures. Two of the girls had absolutely no experience and got far too drunk. After we went back for afternoon classes, one of them threw up at her desk. It didn't take the principal long to unravel what had happened. I was suspended and sent home. My father and stepmother were furious. Mark had a hockey game that night, and the rest of the family was going to go and root for him. My dad said I would learn my punishment when they got home.

As I sat there alone in the house, my head filled with black thoughts. I was a foreigner in that place, as I was everywhere else. The family always went as a group to Mark's games. Only my father had ever come to my basketball games. It was so vividly clear that I wasn't one of them. I was the outsider, the intruder. Once again unloved and unwelcome. The more I sank into my own misery, the less sense it made to wait for a punishment in a house where I wasn't welcome. I went into Danielle's bedroom, took down my Tupac posters, and put everything I owned into my duffel bag. I threw Mark's Discman in with everything else, thinking it would help pass the long bus ride back to Kelowna.

I didn't want to be there when the family got home. I walked to a girlfriend's house to kill time until midnight, when the next bus for Kelowna left the Greyhound station. At eleven, I started walking and eventually hitched a ride to the station. My father and stepmom were waiting for me in front of the ticket windows. They had easily figured out my plan and beat me to the station. Waiting for me to arrive had only made my stepmom angrier. She looked like she could barely stop herself from punching me. She settled for reading me the riot act.

"Who do you think you are? We take you into our home, we feed you. We put up with you. And you pull this?" She went on and on. Finally, she yanked my bag away from me, dropped it to the bus station floor, and unzipped it. She pawed through my stuff, pulling out the Discman. She held it up in my face. "This is how you thank us for letting you into our home? You steal from your stepbrother?" My father stopped her by grabbing her arm. She gave me one last death glare and stormed out to their car.

My father was just as mad, but it was a quieter rage. "You

know, you can come back to our house or you can get on that bus. It's up to you." I might not have been an honors student, but I understood when I was being given a choice that was really a foregone conclusion. There would be no living with my stepmom. My father knew that as well as I did. I had burned that bridge with a white-hot flame. Without so much as a goodbye, I zipped up my bag, shrugged the strap over my shoulder, and walked out to get on the midnight bus to Kelowna.

# -3-

# THE LOST GIRL

T welve is rarely a great age for any girl, but it was an absolute train wreck for me. That was saying something because my life hadn't exactly been rainbows and lollipops before I turned twelve. My mom had moved us in with her new boyfriend, Martin, but the change in housing didn't provide more stability. My mother was too focused on my brother and Martin to pay attention to me, and I would have been a tough kid to wrangle in any case. I ran loose with a small pack of girls from school. We were all terrible students, heavy smokers, and delinquents. There were five of us, including my best friend Jessica, who I'd known since kindergarten. None of us had a positive role model to follow or particularly stable home lives.

I eventually found an even larger tribe to join, a group of preteen and teen girls who gathered outside the bus station in downtown Kelowna. It was a transit hub for the region, so busy that a dozen girls loitering, smoking, and occasionally drinking faded into the background and were invisible to anyone in the crowd of travelers rushing through the station. Unfortunately, we weren't invisible to everyone.

Jason had our number. I can't remember the first time I met him, but he quickly became the pied piper to our group. He was a master puppeteer and he had a grip on all of us. Jason had a particular grifter talent for connecting one-to-one with individual underage girls, making each of us feel special, beautiful, wanted and, yes, even loved. A seasoned street hustler, he possessed near-hypnotic powers over us. It's hard to conceive of now, even for me. Each of us outside that bus station was positive that he was her boyfriend. Any one of us would have done just about anything for Jason.

Anyone with an ounce of common sense would have pegged Jason for the greasy street hustler, pimp, and ex-con he was. Shoulder-length slicked back hair, a mustache and soul patch, and expensive "distressed" clothes. To a gaggle of alienated, confused girls between the ages of twelve and fourteen, he was edgy, cool, and caring. We thought he understood us and cared for us in a way our parents did not. He never showed up without an abundant supply of weed and booze, and freely handed out small amounts of money.

He had a con artist's gift of being able to make you feel ten feet tall. He was that rare beast, an adult who listened to us. That simple ability was incredibly powerful to a group of unheard, unseen outcasts. We had no idea we were being groomed and set up. We were entirely clueless that this criminal was completely the opposite of what he presented himself to be. It wasn't just that we weren't sensible. Certainly, we weren't. It was that we all so badly wanted to buy what he was selling.

He started small, asking one of us to do something illegal like steal some beer or buy cigarettes. Bit by bit, he lured each of us in, making us think that whatever he asked us to do was normal because it came from a loving place. Within a few months, any one of us would have committed a felony for him. We accepted whatever he told us. Like all the girls, I thought he was my boyfriend and that he loved me. Here, finally, was an adult who cared for me, who thought I mattered.

He kept the real love, the unqualified affection that was the emotional opiate my fragile, battered, barely formed ego screamed for, just out of reach. He knew when to reel in a girl like me, someone who was incredibly damaged goods. He understood how to play out the line with a light hand and let the target run. Then he would yank hard and set the hook, gaff the girl and pull her into the boat. He was a pro at sexually manipulating underage girls; we were just young and stupid marks to him. That is the only way I can explain why it was impossible for me to push back when he suggested the unimaginable, the horrific.

"Tiff, I want you to take care of a friend of mine. I need you to show this guy a good time."

"Who is he?"

"Just a guy I know. He's very nice. Make him happy and you'll score a quick hundred dollars."

It was a lot of money. It was a fortune. Far more important, though, Jason wanted me to do this for him. It was impossible to say no. The next day, he drove me to an empty condo on the edge of downtown. The place had no furniture. I met a seventy-year-old man and, without much prelude, we had sex on the floor of one of the empty bedrooms. I felt sick. I turned once again to the faraway numbness that blocked everything, that removed me from the pain and embarrassment. It was an awful moment and I tried to focus on how pleased Jason would be with me. I told myself if I could just get through this, I could get drunk tonight with a pocket full of money and Jason's love securely in my grasp. I focused on anything but the unkempt old man thrusting and grunting on top of me. I never told a soul about that moment, about what happened. Not until I wrote these words.

It seems strange even now to think back to that girl. I can't connect her to me. I can't explain or understand how she fell so deeply into the thrall of an obvious felon, a con man, a pimp. I know others have fallen into the same trap, but I'm certain now that I will never be able to explain to myself or anyone else how or why. Perhaps some dark, evil mysteries are best left unsolved. I know only this. What happened in that bleak, lifeless condo didn't change the way I felt about Jason. It didn't break the hold he had on me. If anything, I had a hundred dollars hidden in a dresser drawer that made me think about him when I got dressed in the morning.

Two days later, Jason spoke to the group of us outside the bus station. He clocked the crowd to be sure that no adult was in earshot and then, talking just loud enough to be heard over the rumble of idling BC transit busses and street traffic, he offered something magical.

"Listen, I want to invite you all to a party I'm having in

Vancouver. We can drink, hang out, and have a blast. It's going to be totally cool. All you have to do is show up here tomorrow at six, and I'm going to have limos bring you to the party. They'll bring you home after it's over."

A limo ride? A party? We were all excited. The idea of a group of outsiders like us being invited to an exclusive event in the adult world, where we would be accepted by "cool" people, seemed too good to be true. I was lucky. If someone was paying for a limo, taking me to a party, it had to mean I was special and that the person accepted me. It was tantalizingly close to being part of a family. A trick of my young, immature mind, but it was no less real for that.

My mother, as it turned out, had not been asleep at the switch. She had already found the money in my dresser drawer when, her antenna raised in high alert, she heard me talking on the phone to another girl. When the word "limos" came up, she did a bit of investigating. She didn't have to dig very deep to discover a group of excited girls who were planning on going to a party. By the time I mustered the courage to tell her I was going on an overnight camping trip with my friends, she had my number.

"Yeah? Are they taking limos to this camping trip?"

I was shocked into silence, and I'm sure my surprise registered on my face. She shook her head. "You're not going anywhere."

Frustration replaced my excitement. Later that night I answered the phone expecting one of the girls from the bus stop calling to tell me how much I was missing out. Instead, it was a woman's voice. She told me she was a friend of Jason's and that he really wanted me to come to the party.

"He's going to miss you if you're not there."

"I want to go. It's just that my mom won't let me."

"She doesn't understand how special this party is. You should sneak out. We'll have you back before she even knows you're gone."

"I'll try."

I didn't, though. Once my mom was on the scent of my wrongdoing, she never let her guard down long enough for me to "sneak out." Besides, the call struck me as strange. For the first time, I began to ask the questions any reasonable person would have asked. Why did Jason have some woman call me? Why was it that important to her that I be there? Even as misguided as I was, as under Jason's influence as I might have been, there was something in the back of my mind that knew that things weren't adding up.

The next day at school, I found out that I was not alone. The news spread like a virus. I discovered that some of the bus station girls had snuck out and made it to the bus station, but had gotten there too late. They returned home, dejected. I felt their sadness and envied the girls who had made it to the bus station by the appointed hour. They were the lucky ones who had been whisked away in the back of long black limos, as if they were movie stars. They had likely enjoyed glasses of cold champagne, because didn't all limos come with champagne? They had partied and had fun, while I stewed in my room, the sound of the TV drifting in from the living room where my warden sat. All day long I envisioned those lucky girls, partying the night away in Vancouver.

I envied them right until the moment I walked into the house after school to find a police detective standing in the living room, talking to my mom. My mother sat absolutely frozen on the beige floral couch, a shocked look on her face. I rapidly searched my mind for things I might have done that would be so illegal as to bring a plainclothes cop to the house. He was tall and thin, with a horse face, but nice in the way adults are to children when they're telling them bad news and have the child's best interests at heart.

I realized my mother wasn't so much angry as stunned. The detective had me sit down next to my mom. He sat across from us and spread a collage of photos out on the coffee table. The photos were of different girls in our group, lounging in front of the bus station. Jason was in some of the images, usually alone with one or another girl. We were laughing and smoking. The photos had obviously been taken at a distance, from a vehicle or building nearby. They seemed like something right out of *NYPD Blue*. I felt sick to my stomach.

The detective looked at me as I looked over the photos. He pointed at Jason. "Do you know this man?" I nodded. I was afraid of saying anything that might make me seem guilty. I certainly wasn't going to tell either my mom or this detective about the old man and the condo. I was scared he'd take me right to jail.

"Did he try to get you to go to a party last night?"

I was stunned. How much did the detective know? I realized that this is what he did for a living. He found things out. I panicked. Maybe he already knew about the old man. I hesitated as he stared at me, unblinking. Then I nodded again.

"He's a very bad guy. Do you know what a pimp is?" I nodded for the third time. "Well, he's a pimp. He has a history of tricking young girls like you into prostitution. You know what a prostitute is, don't you?"

I looked down at the pictures, some of them of me. "Yes."

He paused. "We've arrested him, and we want to arrest some of the people he worked with. If you see an adult that you saw with Jason, I want you to call me.

Okay?"

An image of the old man's face and flabby torso popped into my head as I stared at the photos spread haphazardly across the coffee table. The detective leaned down and locked eyes with me, and my heart skipped a beat.

"Okay?"

I nodded. He scooped up the photos, rapping them on their edges so that they aligned into a neat stack.

"Don't go back to that bus station. We'll be watching it. Call us if any adult approaches you or your friends like this again."

He put a business card on the table where the photos had been. My mom walked him to the door and I went to my room. I now had a word for what had happened with that old man in the condo. I had a word for what Jason was. Oddly, the shame wasn't the worst of it. The most awful part was that I had been abandoned once more. I had never been accepted. Jason didn't love me. It was all a lie and a trick.

The new wave of revelations about Jason's "party" again spread throughout my school. None of us who had gathered outside the bus station wanted to talk about it, and none of us admitted to being invited anywhere. Some of the girls in the detective's photos had gone missing. Two months later, word spread that one of them, a pretty, slender blonde named Olga, had been sold to a brothel in Vancouver. She had tried to escape by jumping from a second-story window, and had broken her leg.

It would have been wonderful if what had happened with Jason had scared us all straight, but it didn't. The four girls in my little posse were all a little wiser and warier once I told them about Jason and the cop, but we were far from reformed. I didn't really appreciate how close to disaster I had come. We continued to spend most of our free time together, smoking, drinking, or doing whatever drugs we could lay our hands on. We barely made it through our classes and shared a total lack of ambition. We all wrestled with weight and body-image issues. We all had negative self-esteem, and a distorted sense of the role sex was supposed to play in our lives. Of the five us, Jessica and I were the tightest. We were pure trouble together.

As I entered my teens, my mother decided I needed professional help and took me to a series of psychologists and therapists. I was diagnosed with ADHD and prescribed a regimen of drugs. I'm not sure what they were supposed to accomplish, but they made me feel like a zombie. The effects were so unpleasant that I stopped taking the pills and they collected in a drawer next to my bed. One night Jessica came over after my mother left to work the swing shift. We sat around my bedroom smoking, and somehow came up with the idea of getting high on my stash of Ritalin.

Instead of getting comfortably buzzed, our pulses raced and

we were borderline delirious. We both felt terrible. At a point, we convinced each other that we should call someone just in case we were in real danger. Although we weren't seriously worried, Jessica's mom understandably freaked out as soon as we told her what we'd done. She called the poison control hotline. They advised her to take us to the emergency room. At the hospital, Jessica and I laughed about the fuss her mom was making. Jessica wound up having her stomach pumped but I got away with a lecture on being more careful with my meds.

For all that, drugs didn't play a significant role in my life. I was never really drawn to them the way some of the kids in the trailer park were. There were other things I thought were more likely to make me cool in the eyes of my friends and peers.

That obsession, my singular focus on what was cool, wasn't just the result of normal teen peer pressure. "Cool" represented something much more all-encompassing and important to me. It was an idea, a word that represented being accepted, admired, and even loved. Cool people were respected and taken seriously. They were the center of attention among their devoted friends. It also meant control—choosing what rules you'd follow and which you wouldn't.

In my thirteen-year-old mind, nothing was more purely cool than a tattoo. I had one in mind. I saw myself impressing all the other kids at school when I pulled up my shirt to show off my shiny new butterfly tramp stamp. I could clearly see that tattoo covering my lower back in glorious, vivid color, just screaming "cool." I was absolutely shocked when my mom said, "Sure," after I asked her if I could get the tattoo.

Two nights later, she and I walked through the door of a dingy little tattoo shop in the seediest part of Kelowna. The "artist" was a gigantic, barrel-chested monster of a man, a bear-sized biker in a leather vest and ponytail. He stunk of sweat and cigarette smoke, mixed with the horseshit tang of pot.

I picked out a butterfly design from his sample book and he printed out a stencil. It looked fantastic in the mirror. The stencil covered the base of my back exactly as I had imagined and I couldn't wait to see the finished tattoo. Getting there, though, was an ordeal. The guy had heavy hands and that tattoo would prove to be one of the most physically painful experiences I would ever experience. Still, I was incredibly happy when he was done. I admired the tat in the morning, turning my head as far as I could over my shoulder to see how the design looked. "Now I'm the coolest kid in school," I thought.

Great in theory, but reality was a letdown. My classmates thought it was a stick-on fake, which sucked a lot of the fun out of the big reveal. The other kids and every adult who saw it wore the same puzzled expression from the one predictable question running through their minds: "Who lets a thirteen-year-old get a tattoo?" I would only truly appreciate the impact of that question after I had my own daughter. In the meantime, I daydreamed about my next tattoo.

Getting inked was and would remain a way to change how I saw myself. I wasn't happy with me or my life. Focusing on my physical appearance was so much easier than attempting to change my life circumstances, behavior, or who I was inside. I wasn't going to suddenly become an honors student or find a new home and family who embraced and loved me unconditionally. But I sure could change the packaging.

My appearance became an even bigger issue in my early teen years because I started gaining weight. I was barely five feet tall, so even a few extra pounds had an impact. And I packed on well more than just a few pounds.

As with any woman who fixates on her physical appearance, it wasn't about how I looked at all. Only much later would I understand that tattoos, tongue piercings, and heavy makeup were misguided attempts at changing myself into someone people would find enticing and worth loving. A new look was my shot at belonging somewhere, of changing my identity. It was a misguided fool's errand, but women a lot older and smarter than I was had fallen into that same trap. The truth that looks aren't the sum of who you are is something I struggle to take on board even now. Maybe more so since I created an avatar who puts bread on my table based purely on the image she projects.

Battles with my weight led to near-constant yo-yo dieting. Nutrition had never been a concern in my mom's household and, truth be told, I usually ate like a garbage panda. Grow up broke and unhealthy food becomes a modest but powerful pleasure in your life. Honestly, the "struggle meals" that were comfort food by another name remain some of my favorite guilty pleasures. There's a part of me that can still experience pure bliss by frying up a piece of bologna and slapping it between two slices of Wonder Bread. Cheese Whiz-and-dill pickle sandwiches were my mom's specialty. One of my earliest, happiest memories is tucking into a bowl of Kraft Dinner with cut-up wieners while I watched *The Little Mermaid* for the hundredth time.

By the time I was fifteen, I didn't have the faintest idea of what constituted a healthy diet. My weight and self-image were all over the map. One day up, one day down. In any given month I might pack on ten extra pounds, losing it a few weeks later with the help of a crazy, unhealthy fad diet.

I was the same age my biological mother had been when she got pregnant with me. I can only guess that was why my adopted mother walked into my bedroom one night and silently dropped a sealed white envelope on my bed, walking out without so much as a word. The envelope contained the only letter my birth mother ever wrote me. It was written in neat, juvenile cursive, and was heartbreakingly simple:

*To my unborn child,*

*This letter will be given to you when you are able to understand what I have to say.*

*If I had a choice, I wouldn't have given you up for adoption. But I had no choice. If I would have kept you, we would have had nothing.*

*When I had you I was only 15 years old and I didn't have a job and I was also living at home. When my parents found out I was pregnant with you, I got moved into an unwed mothers home. They said that even before I got pregnant that if I ever did that I would not be living at home.*

*Your birth father and I did not have a very good relationship at all. Right after we made love, I didn't hear from him for three months. I tried to reach him but I could never get ahold of him. At first when I told him I was pregnant he didn't believe me. He said it must have been someone else but when I told him he was the first boy I was with in over five months he finally believed me.*

*At first I was too scared at the thought of going through 9 months of pregnancy. So I asked my doctor about abortion. Then when the doctor sent me to a specialist to get the abortion, the specialist said I was too far along in the pregnancy to get one done. So then I had to face the fact that I had to go through with it.*

*In the beginning I was scared that something would go wrong and I would feel even worse than if I had gotten the abortion. All through the pregnancy I was scared of that. I fell down the stairs several times and I also fell in the bathtub. For weeks after those accidents I was so careful to be sure that you were all right. Even though I already made my mind up to give you up for adoption, I was still frightened of losing you.*

*I'm going to tell a little about myself so you can get a bit of a picture of what your birth mother was like. I'm approximately 5'6" and I have sandy brown hair and blue eyes. My birthday is on January 17, 1973. I liked to roller skate a lot and draw as a hobby. I really enjoy cooking and cleaning.*

*I also liked to do a lot of things that I wasn't supposed to do. Like going to parties, drinking, etc. In other words, I was testing the world to see just how much I could get away with.*

*Your grandparents names are John and Linda. They got divorced when I was five. Your grandmother got remarried to a man by the name of Doug. Your grandfather remarried when I was 9, her name is Penny. She has two children. Their names are Tryna and Shawna. I have one real brother and his name is Mark. He was thirteen when you were born. When you were born, I lived in Calgary.*

*The reason I picked the parents that adopted you is because they are very loving and great people. I didn't know them personally. But I had a home study done on them. Which is a report on their whole life. It told me if they had a criminal record, what kind of home life they have, and basically what kind of people they are.*

*If you ever need or want to find me, I'll try to be there for you. But just remember that I'm a part of you and will always love you and I'll be in your heart.*

*Love from,*

*Your birth mother*

*Amy XO*

Reading those words made me sadder than I had ever been. I so badly wanted a mother like the woman who wrote that letter, someone who would protect and love me. My adopted mother had done her best, but I keenly felt the reality that her son came first. I was glad to have the letter and some connection to my birth mother, but it also gave me a sense of loss that made my soul ache, like an amputated limb that still hurts long after it's gone.

The only caring person I could turn to in my teens was my adopted grandmother. She was a deeply religious woman, but loved me unconditionally without judging me. It was exactly what I craved because I was such a harsh judge of myself. I needed love and acceptance. The woman who wrote that letter seemed like she would be the type to offer those without hesitation, and my grandmother came a close second. She had her own life, though, and I was always hesitant to bother her with my problems.

Day to day, I felt like I was nobody's concern. In my teen mind, nobody cared, and there was no source of love and comfort. Lacking those, I headed in exactly the wrong direction. I made the all-too-common mistake of thinking attention from men was a measure of my value, and that sex was the same as love. I was searching for validation, acceptance, and proof that I was worth something.

At sixteen, that search took me to the dating website, Plenty of Fish. That's where I met a thirty-year-old named Mateo. He was a heavyset factory worker, a child of Mexican immigrants and a simple, contented person. He had no ambitions beyond getting high when he wasn't working, watching movies, and occasionally having sex. After we started dating, I spent almost every weekend at his rundown apartment. He'd have friends over to party and I'd drink with them and fall asleep next to a much older man who I convinced myself I loved. More to the point, I believed he loved me. I thought I had found my place in the universe. His apartment was a comfortable and welcoming haven for me, especially at a point when I felt increasingly distant from my mother and brother.

Although we hadn't been particularly close before, I could no longer relate to any of the choices my mother was making. She and Martin bonded over a shared interest in Larping—medieval costumed role-playing. They were often gone to large overnight events where people would get drunk on mead and do whatever it is that people drunk on mead do. I found her life impossible to understand.

I think my mother felt like she was running out of road to nail down someone who would support her and be there for the long haul. Martin was a lab technician with a decent savings account. He was a low-maintenance guy who wanted nothing more than to putter with his model trains, work on his cars in the garage, and occasionally dress up and pretend to be a citizen of medieval England. He was a little creepy, but seemed harmless enough.

One Saturday, Mateo was supposed to pick me up but never showed. I was devastated. It wasn't like him to stand me up and I worried that he had dumped me without so much as a "so long" call or text. I rang his cell again and again, leaving voicemail after voicemail. Finally, a woman picked up. She told me she was Mateo's ex-wife and she had some bad news. "Mateo had a heart attack and fell down the stairs. He's dead."

I hung up the phone and sat there trying to process that

reality. How could he have died? Mateo had loved his cocaine and he was far from a healthy guy. Heavy drinking, junk food, and couch living. I understood all that. It's just that in my mind, heart attacks only happened to old people. The loss felt so unfair. I made more of our relationship than it really had been because it was all I had to hold onto. In my head, Mateo had been my once-in-a-lifetime love, a bond that would have lasted forever and ever. His death was one more abandonment. As far as I was concerned, cruel fate had cheated me out of the kind of supportive relationship I craved more than anything.

My family and friends could not understand why I took his death so hard. The truth was that I didn't really understand it either, but I knew that nobody around me was going to help me figure things out. Far from it. Everyone I knew quickly became irritated that I wouldn't let it go.

They felt, rightfully so, that I was wallowing in the pain. I went back to Plenty of Fish to find someone who could absorb the grief or at least distract me from thinking about Mateo. It wasn't long before I connected with a guy named Tim who lived in Vancouver. He played me like a fiddle. He patiently listened while I told him about Mateo and the pain I was going through. There are few things so powerful as someone who doesn't just listen, but really hears you. Tim seemed so understanding, that I didn't think twice when he offered, "Let me bring you out to Vancouver for a weekend and you can forget all about it."

He bought me a Greyhound ticket. I wrote my mom a note that was short on details, left it on the kitchen table under the salt shaker, and headed to the Kelowna bus station.

Tim met me at the bus station at the other end and, even as I walked toward him, I realized I had made a huge mistake. He had stringy, dirty blonde hair, was pale and pasty as an addict, and as purely sleazy looking as a guy could be. He drove us back to his apartment in his ratty twenty-year-old Ford sedan, talking nonstop the whole way. He was an entirely different person than the understanding, respectful listener I had gone back and forth with online.

Once we were inside his sad, dingy apartment, he made it clear that I was now his hostage and I was going to do whatever he wanted. I felt the familiar numbness wash over me. I had screwed up and now I had to focus on escaping and getting myself home. He raped me repeatedly. At one point he made me suck on a pacifier like a baby.

During sex, I slipped away. I wanted so badly just to be home, to be somewhere safe. I wanted to start a new life and leave all my screwups behind. I had made mistakes like this so many times. I just needed a chance to change things. I wondered if I was ever going to get that opportunity.

At one point during the weekend, a neighbor called the cops. A male and female officer showed up at the door. Tim told me not to move from the couch and to keep quiet. The cops came into the apartment and seemed to know that something was up.

"We got a call about noise. Have you two been fighting?"

Without missing a beat, Tim said, "No. It must have been the TV. We've just been hanging out watching movies." I tried to lock eyes with the female officer and signal her that I needed help. She didn't notice. Her partner warned us to keep it down and they left. I was crushed. I had been so close to rescue and now I realized I was going to have to find a way to manufacture my own escape.

That night, Tim fell asleep on the couch after polishing off a bottle of cheap wine. It was clear that I wasn't going to get a better chance to escape.

I quickly and silently gathered my things into my overnight bag. I gently removed my cell phone from the drawer where Tim had put it after demanding I give it to him. I tiptoed to the door, opened it painfully slowly, just enough so that I could slip through the opening. I closed it without making a sound and ran down the street, my bag swinging on my shoulder and pounding my ribs. I ducked behind a dumpster, convinced that Tim would be hot on my trail. I crouched there, shaking, and called the police on my cell. I told the emergency operator what had happened, and she connected me with a police officer.

"You've been kidnapped?"

"I just got away from him. I'm down the block, hiding behind the dumpster. I don't know where I am, but I have to get home to Kelowna."

"Did he kidnap you from Kelowna?"

"No, I came here on the bus. I met him online and came to see him."

There was a long pause. "I'm sorry, but there's nothing we can do."

"He held me prisoner…"

"You came here willingly, right? On a bus? You rode six hours to meet this guy. If we ask him, what's he going to say? It's going to be his word against yours."

I tried not to cry. I didn't know what to say to that. The cop gave me the number for victim's services and hung up.

I was out of options. I called victim services and, after navigating an automated menu, finally got through to a real person. I described where I was and what had happened. After what seemed like an eternity thinking Tim was going to discover me at any minute, take my phone, and drag me back to his apartment, they sent a woman to pick me up. She was a middle-aged lady, kind and radiating calm. I got into the car and we drove to the bus station.

"We called your mother. You need to know that she wasn't thrilled to hear from us. She refused to come get you. I'll buy you a ticket home, but I think you have to be ready for a rough time when you get there. Your mom's really unhappy with you right now."

"I know. I'll make it up to her."

When we got to the station, the woman bought me a ticket on the bus to Kelowna. She wished me luck and left me sitting on a bench waiting for my boarding call. It couldn't come soon enough. I didn't care if my mother yelled at me for hours, or was furious for a month. I just wanted to put as much distance as possible between me and that creep. I wanted to go to sleep in my own bed and not think about anything. In a way, the trip had achieved its goal; Mateo was the last thing on my mind.

The bus ride went on forever. Mile after desolate mile rolled past my window and I started to relax. Finally, we pulled into the Kelowna bus station. I called my mother who refused to pick me up. In fact, she told me I would have to find somewhere else to live.

"You can't come back here. This is just too much. I've done everything I can, but I'm through."

"What am I supposed to do? Where do I go now?"

"I found a women's shelter that has a bed for you. Go stay there and figure it out." She gave me the address and hung up before I could think of anything else to say. I stood in front of the bus station trying to process everything that had happened in the short span of a few days. I had made a lot of mistakes in a small amount of time and I was flat out of options. I picked up my bag and started hitchhiking, eventually catching a ride across town to the address my mother had given me.

I got out of the car and stood there taking in the single-story brick building. It wasn't pretty, and it was smack on a noisy main street. I didn't recognize the area.

I was lost in every way you can be lost. This ugly, squat building in front of me was the only place between me and sleeping on the street. I was sixteen years old. I had no boyfriend, no job, and no money. My grandmother might have helped, but I had put myself in this situation and had no right to burden her. I had no friends who would take me in. I felt as unloved, unwanted, abandoned, and alone as a person can be. I walked around to the main door of the Alexandra Gardner Women and Children Safe Centre. Right before I opened it, I thought, "I guess now I'm homeless."

# -4-

# DESPERATELY SEEKING FAMILY

F ind yourself in a homeless shelter and you quickly realize
that it's either going to be a stop on the road to someplace
a whole lot worse, or a Godzilla-size wake-up call. It was
the second one for me. I had to get my shit together. I was too
young to wind up camping in a cardboard box on the streets of
Kelowna. For the moment, I had a bed, food, and a roof over my
head. That was a start. I was damn good and well going to use
that sobering experience to take some control over my life and
put my fate in my own hands.

At sixteen, I was the youngest resident in the Centre. I was
also—even for all my bad decisions—the most stable person
there. The other women had all hit rock bottom. Many were
prostitutes and most were addicted to drugs, alcohol, or both. I
was not an unwed pregnant teen, a crack addict, or a prostitute.
That made me the gold star resident.

Here's the thing, though. Talk to a person every day, hear her stories, share her laughter and tears, and you see that person as she truly is—just another human being. The labels society or other people slap on someone aren't the sum of that person's identity. Labels aren't who we really are. That should be obvious, but it took living at a shelter for me to really grasp that truth.

Every one of us has hopes and fears. We all want to be safe, loved, and happy. Some of us lose our way and can't for the life of us figure out how to find those things. We settle for shallow replacements—drugs, sex, abusive relationships—for happiness. Finding security and joy is a huge challenge in the best of times, but once conventional society has decided you're a "junkie," a "drunk," or a "hooker"? Well, then, it's damn near impossible.

Maybe I wasn't battling the type of life-and-death problems and demons the other women were, but I could still empathize. Compassion came naturally because, at the shelter, I was just one more member of a big, strange family. Sure, it was a dysfunctional family, but what family isn't?

The place we all called "home" was anything but homey. Just the same, I was comfortable there. Everyone had to check in and out with the manager on duty who sat in a small, locked office just inside the entrance. That was also where residents picked up their prescription meds. The large, central living room was furnished for relaxing, with a huge black, well-worn sectional couch and a few beat-up easy chairs that invited you to sprawl. It was the most popular place in the shelter because it had the only TV. There was a small kitchenette where anyone could grab a snack, coffee, or soda, and a separate fully equipped kitchen that the staff used to prepare meals for everyone. The kitchen shared a pass-through window with a big, well-lit dining room where we ate dinner together every night.

My favorite spot was the room I shared with a woman named Molly. She spent most of her time in the living room, so the spare little box of a room was a happy sanctuary where I could find solitude almost anytime I needed it. The room had battered blue-grey walls and a window that caught the morning sun. Like all the rooms in the shelter, it wasn't meant to seem permanent, so it was barely furnished. There were two folding cots, a beat-up wood dresser we shared, and a metal gym locker for each of us.

Molly, like all the women at the shelter, had fascinating and heartbreaking stories to tell. She was an alcoholic who had been physically abused by every man she had ever known. Her husband had done a number on her before she finally left him. She was trying to figure out the next steps in her life. Molly had a frenzied way of talking, a wild mane of curly black hair, a constantly startled expression, and nervous tics. She seemed way too shell-shocked to have much of a chance of moving forward.

One of my favorite women at the shelter, Laurie, had been a successful lawyer in Toronto. Weekend heavy partying had grown into a full-blown heroin addiction. Her drug use had cost her everything. She had lost her home, her career, her family and friends, and her reputation. Even her looks had paid the price. She had obviously once been beautiful, but now looked grey and haggard, and ten years older than she really was.

Regardless of all that, Laurie was a walking example of the power of hope. In spite of her history, of how far she had fallen, she held a dogged faith in the future, an optimism that she could rebuild her life. Her hope was infectious. If, after all the mistakes she had made, Laurie could still see a bright future, there had to be a chance for me.

Sadly, most of the other women didn't dare look so far ahead. Hope and dreams could be risky. The majority of the shelter's residents were overwhelmed with just making it through another day. Delores was typical of the broken souls there. She said she was sixty-five, but looked as old as time. Toothless and fantastically wrinkled, she was the mother hen among the residents. Everyone called her "Ma" because she checked in with each of us on a regular basis, making sure we were all okay. She couldn't show herself the same kindness, and would wind up dying alone on the street, less than a year later.

The stories went on and on and they all broke my heart. Maria was a young mother of three, and had lost custody of her kids because of an all-consuming crack habit. Angie was a schizophrenic who had suffered unspeakable traumas and battled horrifying ghosts no one else could see. She had to choke down a handful of powerful meds every day just to function at the most basic level.

One of my best friends in the shelter was a pregnant woman named Belinda. Short like me, she was quick with a joke and had a beautiful smile. Seven months into her pregnancy she was battling a crack addiction and losing. She was, like so many others there, a walking contradiction. She didn't want to hurt her unborn baby any more than she wanted to live penniless in a women's shelter. She loved the child inside her. It was plain to see that her heart was in the right place and she had an undeniable sweetness. It was just that she was incredibly sick and didn't have the strength or support network to get well. That meant that she was likely going to continue risking her baby's shot at life and destroying her own.

I felt the pain and struggle each and every one of them was going through. Sure, they were flawed, but so was everyone I had ever known. So was I. We all have our ugly sides and broken parts. Those women were just more flawed than most people. That didn't mean they didn't deserve decent lives or basic happiness. They craved the simple things most people take for granted: a place to lay your head down where there was no curfew. A way out of the pain, and some sense that the future might be better than today. Instead, they settled for a role in our small misfit tribe, and the simple structure and routines we all followed to make some sense of each day, one day at a time.

Every morning, we would grab mugs that had been used by scores of women before us, and fill them with brutally strong hot coffee. We'd head out to the back courtyard where each of us would post up in one of the many weather-beaten, aluminum-framed patio chairs. Everyone would make small talk and share a few jokes, smoking the first cigarettes of the day. After breakfast, everyone had to leave the shelter until five. Most of the women didn't have jobs, and I wasn't sure where they went. Some worked as prostitutes. I had a job cleaning hotel rooms. I'd landed the gig the first week I was at the shelter and I was the only resident who had a regular job.

Buzzing from the jolt of caffeine and nicotine, I'd head inside, make my lunch, and walk to the bus stop. I'd catch the BC Transit

Number 10 line downtown. It felt good to be busy and to have somewhere to go every day. On Fridays I'd hand my paycheck over to the shelter manager. She would put it in an envelope and lock it in the office safe, and I'd go to sleep one step closer to having my own place.

Every night, all the residents sat down together for a communal dinner. That hour in the dining room was when I most felt like I was part of a family. I loved the sounds of knives and forks clacking against plates, the smell of cheesy enchiladas or beef stew filling the room. It was lovely to hear the music of women talking over one another and laughing at each other's jokes. For the briefest moment, we were all fine. A group of lovely faces happily animated in the fading late spring light streaming through a dining room window.

We were an odd little temporary sorority. We didn't talk about it, but the emphasis was on "temporary." Residents were only allowed to stay for thirty days. The shelter management made an exception for me because I was so young and had a job and a plan. It didn't matter that we weren't going to be together long term.

We were more than just random women lumped in a group. We shared everything, from small personal dramas to our weekly rituals. We'd gossip like sisters over our morning smokes and argue heatedly once a week for our chosen champions on *American Idol*. It was impossible not to care about each other. We had all made awful mistakes. We had little to offer, but we gave each other the simple grace of understanding, and a space to be flawed but accepted.

That bond made Thursday the roughest day of the week. Welfare checks came on Wednesday, and the money created a terrible temptation to backslide into partying and the dark life that had brought most of us to the shelter in the first place. The rules, however, were strict: miss curfew, lose your bed. Every Wednesday, a few of our tribe would go out the door, never to return. I spent most Thursday mornings hunkered down in the courtyard, listening to the birds as I took long drags from my cigarette and wondered where the missing ones were. Where did they spend the night? Were they okay? Had they OD'd? Did something terrible happen to them? Everyone in the courtyard would be unusually quiet on Thursday mornings. There were a lot of glum faces and thousand-yard stares.

After two and half months and watching a dozen women lose their beds and never come back, I had finally saved up enough money to rent my own apartment. It was a simple thing, but it seemed like a huge accomplishment. I felt like I had climbed a mountain. I found a tiny studio near the center of town.

The night before I moved out, Laurie came strutting into the living room with good news of her own. Her years of heroin use had ruined her teeth, but she had just come from the dentist who had given her all new veneers. She was beaming and her smile looked gorgeous. It was a big step back toward her old life, and she talked excitedly about how good it felt to be able to smile again without feeling self-conscious. Everyone in the room knew exactly what that meant. Laurie was wiped out from the anesthesia the dentist had given her, so we hugged and she headed off to bed to get a good night's sleep.

The next morning, she didn't show up in the courtyard for our morning smoke. I finished my coffee and went in to look for her to say goodbye. I found her still in her bed. She had died sometime during the night. It was a horrible blow and an incredibly painful reminder of the cruel lives every woman in the shelter had lived and continued to face. One more lesson in just how bitterly unfair fate could be. Laurie had been so happy and hopeful the night before. I think new teeth were a tangible sign that maybe she could one day again practice law, her bid to get back to "normal." She had been cheated out of what might have been. I never found out what killed her, but her death was a final bit of sadness to take with me, the worst of my memories from the shelter.

My new home was on the second floor of a century-old building. There were nine units, all alike. Once upon a time they would have been called "single room occupancy" or SROs, and rented nightly or weekly to transients and drifters. The current state of the building wasn't much of an improvement. My apartment was two hundred square feet covered in the most horrid green carpet known to man. There was a persistent smell of Chinese takeout and stale smoke. I had a hot plate and a bachelor mini-fridge, and a bathroom about the size of what you'd find on a plane. There were, however, two glorious sun-filled windows and, after I paid the rent, I could go to sleep knowing that no one could throw me out. It was my fortress, my palace, and mine alone. It was home.

The other tenants were a rough crowd. Addicts crowding four

to a studio apartment, headed down life's ladder to shelter living or worse. A cast of generally sketchy characters was always lurking about. I always locked my door whether I was inside the apartment or not.

The neighbors didn't change anything for me; I absolutely loved my dumpy little hole in the wall. That apartment was a step in the right direction as far as I was concerned, even if I was still in pure survival mode. I hadn't learned how to plan for the future and hope was still a risky bet. I was happy enough just to come home from work every day, sit out on the overhang under *my* windows, smoke cigarette after cigarette, and daydream about being skinny, pretty, and rich. Occasionally, I'd go out with Jessica and the other girls and get up to some of my old hijinks. We'd drink and gossip for a couple hours. Then I'd come home to my tiny safe haven and fall asleep in my twin bed with its lumpy mattress. I had dropped out of high school as a junior, so I slowly worked my way through the correspondence coursework toward my GED.

Life was good. Certainly better than at a shelter. Even losing my job wasn't a damper on the positive feeling. I lost it the same way I did all my minimum wage jobs: indifference and laziness. I had a late night with my girlfriends and just didn't feel like getting up in time to make it to work. Two unexcused absences later, the manager called. "Don't bother coming back." It wasn't a setback.

Young and rash, I knew there were plenty of crappy minimum-wage jobs around. All of them were boring or outright unpleasant and the people in charge were inevitably disrespectful and full of themselves. I didn't worry that I'd have any trouble finding work or that I was putting myself at risk of heading back to a shelter. In fact, it took me less than two days and little effort to find my next job as a cashier at Bubbles, "The Champagne of Car Washes."

It was a busy place and the days went by quickly. I continued to battle weight and self-esteem issues, so I got little attention—wanted or unwanted—from co-workers or the men who brought their cars in to be washed. The one exception was the day manager, Bobby.

He was a native Canadian, with light brown skin, a round face, peaked eyebrows, and a gap-toothed smile. He reminded me of a Jack-O-Lantern every time he smiled at me. He found a lot of excuses to spend time near the cashier counter. Finally, two of the girls who worked at the car wash took me aside and told me that Bobby liked me. They asked me what I thought of him. I said that he seemed nice, which he did. I had a hard time believing anyone could really have a crush on me, so I didn't think much about it. A week later, Bobby asked me out.

We were both poor so we didn't so much date as hang out. No softly lit restaurant meals or long romantic walks along the lakeshore at sunset for this girl. We'd split a pizza and sit on his well-worn couch watching movies on pirated cable. Bobby lived in a much nicer part of town, in a much better apartment. He wasn't anybody's idea of Prince Charming, but then again, I didn't feel like anyone's idea of a princess. Besides, it was an easy relationship because Bobby so obviously adored me from day one. He didn't see the fat girl or the lazy cashier, or the high school dropout who had spent two months in a women's shelter. He saw a different woman, and she made him happy. It felt good to be seen as that woman.

Each of us falls into a trap of thinking our identity is this one thing, how you view yourself, however you define *you*. Really, though? That's far from the whole picture. Everyone in your life colors you with a different identity. The girl Bobby saw when he looked at me wasn't the insecure overweight chick I faced down in the mirror every morning. I'll admit I liked that he saw another, better me. It was flattering that he was so obviously crushing on that girl. When I was around him, I could almost believe I was her. I told myself I loved him too, even though I didn't. It was a convenient lie, especially for someone who felt like she was unlovable and would never in her life get another chance to land an adoring suitor.

I had just turned seventeen when we met. Our bare-bones courtship lasted almost two years, at which point I decided that I wanted to be married as soon as I was legally allowed to. Partly, I saw it as the next step on the way to some notion of family, but it was also a cold calculation on my part. Bobby had developed a painfully obvious puppy crush on the blonde floozy who lived upstairs, and I was having none of that. I had been pleasantly surprised anybody would fall in love with me, and I wasn't going to lose what looked to be my one shot at a lasting relationship. It meant I had to lock him down. Canadian law required waiting until my nineteenth birthday.

My mother had married Martin the year she kicked me out. Maybe it was regret, or her way of trying to bridge the gap between us, but she couldn't have been more supportive of her nineteen-year-old daughter getting hitched. That surprised me. Somewhere deep down I knew that I was too young and immature to get married. Bobby and I didn't have anything you could call prospects for the future, and we were literally living paycheck to paycheck. My mom, though, wanted to help.

"Why don't you have the wedding in our backyard? That'll be our gift to you."

We didn't have money for a church wedding and a reception, so a backyard barbecue was the only alternative to a basic ten-minute City Hall ceremony. The backyard was a handsome suburban outdoor space. Well-tended, short-cropped lawn covered what the swimming pool didn't. There were a few flowering plants and fruit trees along the edges. It was small but tidy. My adopted dad's mother shocked the hell out of me by sending a thousand-dollar check as a wedding present. I spent two hundred on the cheapest white bridal gown I could find and deposited the rest. It was the most money Bobby or I had ever had in the bank at one time.

I never imagined that I would actually find someone who loved me enough to marry the woman I knew I was. That made the wedding a magical moment for me, even if it was a touch white trashy. My mom had done her best. We were married in front of thirty guests sitting in folding chairs set up in a grid on the lawn. Jessica was my maid of honor. I wore my birth mother's pearls; her mother had come to the wedding and given them to me. My stepfather had cleaned the small swimming pool and it looked exceptionally blue and sparkly under the bright spring sun. The fruit trees were in bloom and the entire backyard was decorated with white-and-purple flowers and bunting.

A local Justice of the Peace married us, and was surprised to find that Bobby and I had both already gotten matching wedding ring tattoos. After the ceremony, we blasted Lynyrd Skynyrd and served barbecued burgers and hot dogs. We cut a store-bought sheet cake, had a toast, and headed off to our honeymoon of one night in the best room on offer at the local Super 8 motel.

It was all over and done so quickly. I had naively imagined that getting married would be a magic wand waved over my life, changing everything for the better. A week later, I was disappointed to find nothing had changed. I didn't feel any different. Our jobs were the same, the apartment was the same. We were still broke, parking on the same couch, eating the same fast-food dinners. I had that overwhelming feeling people often experience when they dream about going someplace new for so long that they build it up in their minds. They create a mystical, fantasy location. When they finally arrive, there's the unique disappointment of, "Oh … it feels just like any other place."

Life continued on in survival mode. We struggled and struggled and didn't have a pathway to something better because neither of us were qualified for more rewarding jobs or had been the type of student who might be able to find a way back to college and a career.

My mom and Martin threw us a bone, renting us the tiny, weather-beaten freestanding apartment in their backyard. They charged us a token three hundred per month. It was a welcome break from what we had been paying, but it meant dealing with domestic dramas on an ongoing basis. I would often have morning tea with my mom for a week straight. Then we would have a blowout fight about nothing, each of us so good at pushing the other's buttons. We would avoid each other for a week or more. It was, as always, a rollercoaster with my mom. One day she showed up at my door, breathless. I thought, "Oh boy, here we go again."

"I need your help."

"What's going on?"

"I think Martin's been spending time on dating websites, but I don't know how to get into his computer. You know about this stuff. Can you see if he's cheating on me?"

I wasn't particularly close to my stepfather and if I could stop him from screwing over my mother, I was up for that. "Okay, let's check it out."

She sat me down in front of his off-brand laptop. It wasn't password protected and took me less than a minute to open his search history. Martin had always struck me as a slightly creepy guy so I figured my mom might be right. The reality was worse than any dating site. He had been cruising hardcore porn sites, many that featured underage girls. I showed my mom some of the pages he had visited and she went pale. "I thought he was just cheating on me...."

"Mom, some of this is child porn. You understand? These aren't just women, they're little girls. You've got to report him to the police. You know that, right?"

She nodded. I could see that she was in shock. It crossed my mind that she might be overwhelmed with the reality of what we found and would hesitate to turn Martin in. So as soon as I got back to the apartment, I called the police and told them what I had found. They arrested Martin at work. I went over the next day to let my mom know I would support her and help her move out. I was stunned when she told me that she planned on staying put. "I talked to a divorce lawyer. He told me if I moved out, I'd lose the chance to get a piece of the house in the divorce."

The house. Money, property, stuff. I'd seen my mom make some questionable decisions over time, but I simply couldn't understand how she could be willing to stay with a pedophile just in the hope of getting what she thought was coming to her. I disliked Martin, but he had owned that house for years before he met my mother. He had always paid the bigger share of the bills. Regardless of the circumstances, I didn't feel my mom had a right to his money or his house. Besides, who would willingly keep living with a degenerate like that?

As desperate as I was to get out of poverty, that was a line I would not cross; I was incredibly disappointed that my mother would. Her mind was clearly made up and I lost a lot of respect for her because of it. In the end, all I could do was make my own decisions, which meant getting the hell away from that house.

It took me two days to find us a place on the other side of town for twelve hundred dollars a month. It was a lot more than we could afford, but I wanted to move before Martin made bail and came home. I lied my ass off on the application and by the end of the week we had moved into our new thousand-square-foot home. I felt a lot safer, even though the higher rent made our financial situation much more precarious. Actually, precarious would be putting it mildly.

Five months later, I kicked things up a notch in spite of our money problems. In another misguided attempt at trying to create radical change in pursuit of a new and better life, I decided to get pregnant. I saw it as the door to the happy, warm place I'd been searching for forever. I was sure that this time it would surpass my expectations, that having a child would be the real earthshaking difference that would deliver a shiny new reality.

Who can explain the wonky logic of a teenager trapped in her own misery? Somehow, I convinced myself that a baby would create the loving, accepting dream family I never had growing up. Flawed as that reasoning might have been, it was even stranger given I had never particularly wanted kids or thought about becoming a mother.

Bobby didn't question my decision. He took it in stride and I got pregnant within a week of deciding that's what I was going to do. After an argument with the top boss at the car wash, I quit and took a new job as an auto parts delivery driver. That one came to an abrupt end after the chubby-chasing manager shoved his hand down my pants. Next up was a counter position at a fast food place called Taco Time. The supervisor liked to shout at everyone working there, but I became her favorite target. The final straw was her threat to dunk my head in the deep fryer for messing up an order. I quit on the spot and got hired the next day at the local Subway.

Bobby and me, we barely scraped by. We might have been working but we weren't earning a living. The expensive townhouse was sucking us dry and we were stuck in a lease. We could have managed to bump along given that we were so used to living below the poverty line, but it wasn't just us anymore. Everything was becoming so deadly adult, taking on a brutally serious edge as my belly ballooned with this baby.

Every quiet moment was filled with panic. I would be on a break outside the sandwich shop, staring off into a cloud-dappled sky. My mind would race, and I would think, "I shouldn't have done any of this. How could I be married? Pregnant? I'm nineteen years old for fuck's sake. What do I know about giving a baby what it needs, giving it love or creating a family? I've never had a real family...." Those horrible thoughts popped up one after another inside my head with no way to stop them. I was increasingly certain that I had made absolutely the biggest mistake of an already bungled life. What could I do, though, so far past the point of no return?

Delivery day loomed. A week before the due date, I quit Subway. I waited and waited. Three days overdue, my doctors decided to break my water and induce labor. It was a quick two-hour labor, but a rough, agonizing birth. The pain was worse than I had imagined pain could be. I would have taken anything they gave me, but drugs were out of the question because the labor progressed so quickly. Isabella emerged weighing seven pounds, nine ounces.

I felt terrible afterward, exhausted, and sickened physically and mentally. They sent me home the next day, but I developed a high fever. It stumped the doctors until they discovered a raging blood infection. They readmitted me and I spent a week in the hospital being pumped full of intravenous antibiotics. Between the sickness, my lingering doubts about motherhood, and what I would only much later understand was postpartum depression, I couldn't connect in a meaningful way with the baby that the hospital kept in a bassinette beside my bed. That disconnect made me feel worse about myself in what was a circle of misery.

It would take me the longest time to bond with my daughter. Even after I came home from the hospital, I was completely disassociated from Izzy. It was the strangest feeling. I added to the many faults I saw in myself, "shitty mom." I had the overwhelming feeling that Izzy had nothing to do with me. She was just a bundle of cells, a living organism I knew I was supposed to care for. I didn't feel the motherly love I had heard about and seen in feel-good, made-for-TV movies. I wasn't up to taking care of her. I could barely care for myself. I just wanted to go to sleep and wake up a long time in the future, in a better place.

I didn't want to be married anymore, or a mother, or responsible for anything or anyone. I would have given up a limb to have everything just go back to the way it had been before I met Bobby. I fantasized about being home alone in that tiny studio with its incredibly ugly green rug. Thankfully, Bobby was an excellent father from the start. He picked up the slack and shouldered most of the burden of caring for our newborn, while I worked my way through the fog in my brain and the stupefying emotional numbness.

We had other problems, too. The three of us couldn't possibly make it on what Bobby earned at the car wash. We signed up for government assistance. It was, more than anything else, incredibly embarrassing. I lined up outside the food bank every Tuesday morning, standing there with all these other people who were so obviously miserable. My heart would go out to them and I would feel like a fraud. I had seen the darkest that bottom could be in the stories the women at the shelter told me. I imagined that the people around me were in circumstances like that, far worse off than Bobby and I were. Some of the people in that line were likely homeless.

Shifting from foot to foot as I waited in the middle of the gritty, desolate parking lot outside a faceless warehouse in a stark, industrial part of town, I felt so ashamed. It was yet one more place I didn't belong. I would often think, "What went so wrong in my life that I'm waiting in a line outside this rundown, dusty building for the chance to pick up a week's worth of diapers and rummage through a bin of rotting vegetables?" It was dehumanizing. I felt even worse because I knew I had only myself to blame.

The self-loathing and doubts were another part of the postpartum depression I struggled with for weeks. That disease is like being buried under a smothering pile of blankets that are invisible to everyone around you. I felt like I couldn't breathe or see the sun. At certain moments, I was incapable of doing anything. Brushing my teeth was sometimes a goal I couldn't imagine conquering.

My obstetrician had been keeping tabs on me after the blood infection and I finally opened up to her about the vague group of symptoms for which I didn't yet have a name. She gave me the diagnosis of postpartum depression, explaining in detail the cause of symptoms I so clearly had. She wrote me a prescription for strong antidepressants.

Within a couple of weeks, the debilitating emotional paralysis began to fade. Little by little the fog lifted and I established an actual bond with Izzy, one that grew stronger every day. I saw now that she was more beautiful than the most perfect night sky full of luster-dust stars. More beautiful than a bright rainbow or a fabulous, brilliantly colored painting.

She stuck her hand up into the air and grabbed at nothing just to discover what grabbing was, and in those unsteady fingers she held all of my heart. I realized then, right at that moment, that the terrifying ice wall of postpartum depression was melting. I could see her in all her perfection and I became her mother in every sense of the word. I was Tiffany, once Samantha, and soon to be Jessica. Most of all, though, most importantly of all, I was Izzy's mom. This wonderful tiny little human. I'd hold her and look into her eyes, and be awestruck. She was my family. I knew that unique love now. I got it. I could feel it. I decided that come hell or high water I was going to create a great life for this little girl. A wonderful place in the universe where we both could live.

It made me think of what my birth mother had wanted for me. I couldn't talk to her or touch her, and Izzy would never meet her, but it dawned on me that none of that was true about my biological father. The more I considered it, the more I thought I had to find him. Who knew? Maybe he would regret not being there for me. Perhaps he could be a wonderful addition to Izzy's life. A grandfather who would adore her as I did. I wanted to find him for me, as well. Out there, somewhere, was my real father. We were linked by the blood that pumped through our veins. He had a daughter he might not even know existed. What if he had looked for me, wondering the many "what if's" that I did? He could be a powerful piece of the family puzzle I wanted to assemble, just waiting to take his place in our lives.

I turned to social media. I spent hours hunting down my birth mother's high school classmates, emailing or texting them one by one. I asked each one if they remembered who my mom was dating around the time I would have been conceived.

Most were entirely gracious in their replies, but no one seemed to have any idea who my father could have been. Finally, a woman named Elizabeth responded. She was certain she knew who my father was. She remembered a boy dating my mother, and then breaking it off right when my mother got pregnant. Elizabeth even remembered his name.

I found him on Facebook, and Elizabeth called him and let him know who I was. I sent him a friend request and he accepted it. He wasn't quite what I expected and his profile picture made him look like a pretty dubious character, with a scraggly goatee, shaved head, and neck tats. I should have been the last person to judge any book by its cover, but he struck me as someone potentially dangerous.

I was hesitant about going any further, and leery of starting a dialog. I decided that I'd wait for him to reach out to me and see how I felt then. I waited a week, then two, with no contact. Finally, I decided to unfriend him. Discovering him turned out to be enough; it provided all the closure I needed. I was leery of opening a Pandora's box, of finding out things I might not want to know. I had enough challenges in my life. At least I knew his identity and how to reach him in the future, if I ever wanted Izzy to meet him.

In the meantime, I had bigger fish to fry. I was pondering my birth mother's life. How awful it must have been at the point when she gave me up. I understood, now, how it would kill a part of me to do that. How far down I would have to be to ever let Izzy go. I realized I had to make some radical changes. I needed to come up with some sort of realistic plan for the future.

First and foremost, if I was going to believe in myself and get things done, I had to shed the extra sixty pounds I had been carting around forever and a day. As soon as I did that, I would feel confident enough to take Izzy and leave Bobby. He hadn't done anything wrong. In fact, his only crime was being an incredible father and loving his wife and daughter. The harsh truth was that I just didn't love him. I couldn't imagine spending the rest of my life with him. He wasn't as hungry as I was to break out of our life, out of our circumstances. I was going to do whatever it took to escape poverty. I didn't want to struggle constantly. I was going to have a better, brighter life, and I was going to give that life to my daughter.

As refreshing as it was to have a clear direction, to feel like I was taking initiative, the question inside my head remained, "How the hell am I going to do all that? I have no money, no skills, no place to go, no help." I decided that all I could do was tackle one thing at a time.

First, I picked up a dust-covered case of vanilla SlimFast shakes from the food bank. They launched me on my way down the long road to skinniness. Unfortunately, the weight loss didn't happen nearly fast enough for my liking. In yet another bad decision, I decided to speed up the process with a dark secret that

I would never tell anyone. I became bulimic. I can't recall the moment I came upon the idea, or what inspired it. Somewhere, somehow, I realized that if I just threw up after a meal, I could enjoy whatever I wanted to eat and still lose weight at a fast clip. I could literally have my cake and eat it, too.

Bulimia is the illusion of control. It becomes a ritual that allows you to feel even better than you would if you had exercised will power and just hadn't eaten. Of course, there are the dark moments on the other side of that feeling, where you ask yourself, "Shit, why did I do that. Why? Why do I keep doing this?" It's not so much shame as disappointment with yourself.

Still, as it would so often in the future, bulimia seemed like the perfect solution for my immediate goals. I rapidly shed the weight I wanted to lose, while indulging the bad foods that made me feel good for a moment. I still ate packages of cookies, burgers, Kraft Dinners with cut-up wieners—and never paid the price. Or so I thought. Bulimia is just payment deferred. I'd find that out much later when I forked out a small fortune for veneers to repair the damage caused by years of stomach acid gushing over my teeth. For the moment, though, I thought I'd found my holy grail of weight loss.

The next item on my short to-do list was finding a place to land once I left Bobby. I would have to move out if I was going to move on. One morning, I bundled Izzy up in a hand-me-down snowsuit and drove my Neon to the local social services office to apply for public housing. The woman across the desk looked over my application, nodded, and punched me in the face with a harsh dose of reality.

"This all looks good. I'll put you on the list."

"List?" I had assumed that Izzy and I would have our own apartment within a couple of weeks. "How long is the list?"

"Right now, the wait is about two years."

I walked out of the office knowing that I had to manufacture some sort of opportunity that would get me where I was going quicker than that. Two years might as well have been a hundred. I couldn't stay in a holding pattern that long. I was fed up with my life. Being unemployed and on public assistance gives a girl a lot of time to think about big changes and new directions. I had no real skills to speak of. I was losing weight at a fast clip, so at least I was doing something right. I needed a bigger idea, something that wouldn't just be an answer, but would be *the* answer.

I wasn't focusing on the fact that I had done a lot of damage. I had hurt Bobby in ways you should never hurt another person, and now it was his turn to wrestle with debilitating depression. In the midst of my "new life" campaign, he had what I could only call a breakdown. He quit his job at the car wash and began sleeping sometimes ten hours at a stretch. He needed to wake up to someone who was being supportive, someone who made a concerted effort to understand what he was going through and helped him. That wasn't me.

We didn't have the resources to get him the mental health care he needed, and he didn't have a wife who loved and supported him through his personal crisis, so he was left to find his own way through. It would be a few years before he would discover his version of happiness and balance. In the moment, the best he could muster was the occasional odd job or temporary position. He tried to sell vacuum cleaners, but he was no salesman. He dropped off resumes at various stores in town, but never got called back for an interview. Finally, without saying it out loud, he gave up. I'm sure I played a big role in what was clearly deep clinical depression.

Together, we added up to a real mess. I was profoundly unhappy and now so was he. We had only public assistance to pay the bills and it was far from enough. We were stressed and lost. I realized that in trying to find an escape, I had only made everything worse. Our financial situation continued to deteriorate. We were in real trouble in every way two full-grown immature adults and a baby could be. The mess our lives had become and the fear of what loomed in the months ahead led me to worry night and day.

I fought it almost non-stop, that ink-black anxiety. It dogged me even as I pushed Izzy in her stroller toward my car. We had just spent yet another dispiriting Tuesday morning at the food bank. We were in sight of the Neon when one of the hinges on the stroller disintegrated. There was no way to keep the damn thing open, much less roll it forward. The frustration welled up as I unbuckled Izzy, rested her on my hip, and left the useless junk stroller behind. As I angrily buckled Izzy into her seat, I thought, "Fuck. This is just what I needed, one more thing to go wrong." I was yet to learn—but soon would—that every problem is just an opportunity in disguise.

# -5-

## CAMMED IF I DO

C amming is a bizarre business. It's not just the screwy concept of complete strangers paying you to connect with them sexually, emotionally, and socially through the screen of a computer, tablet, or phone. Sure, that's odd. The weirder part, though, is what happens on the business end of a webcam. I never actually saw my clients. I'd stare at a computer screen and the video feed of myself, and I'd have no proof that there was anyone on the other side except for a comment window filling with text. That was a blessing. Still, imagination never hesitates to venture into the unknown. My mind filled in the blanks as I formed distinctive mental images of—identities for— my regulars.

I had some clients who were, let's say, swimming out of the mainstream. One guy liked to have a long conversation in private chat while I sat in front of the camera with bright orange processed cheese slices on my naked boobs. Another paid me to chug a large bottle of soda and belch loudly. A particularly disconcerting client just wanted me to hunch over faced away from the camera, so that he could get his jollies while focusing on the curve of my naked spine. I wouldn't even realize he had soundlessly dropped out of the chat until I sat there for five minutes like an idiot.

I went along with it all; these guys paid the bills and then some. I avoided judgments like "weird." Who decides what's "normal" when it comes to sexual preferences, anyway? I wasn't going to criticize; my cam page was a safe zone. I wanted my clients to enjoy themselves.

The experience wasn't the same for me. Camming was never once even close to pleasurable. At best, it was the physical equivalent to cleaning my ears with a cotton swab. I was self-conscious the entire time I was on camera. Did I have the right angle? Do I have a roll here, or is that side unflattering? You have to be performer, director, video editor, and grip all in one. It's a lot of work and exhausting. I was completely spent after two hours on camera.

There were also safety concerns. Cam girls inevitably have to deal with stalkers. The wrong guy can easily assume that because you pay close attention to him, he owns you. Those guys often become unreasonably and sometimes dangerously jealous. The idea was always to give every client the girlfriend experience and establish a rapport over time. Sometimes, though, a guy would think he was actually my boyfriend and get furious that I showed any attention to other cam customers. I learned to be careful and nip any trouble in the bud. It meant letting problematic clients down easy, but I eventually always had to block them.

The potential for a dangerous stalker was something I took seriously. I blocked my location, never gave out my "real" name (although, ironically, Jessica Wilde became my real name), and tried never to reveal that I was Canadian. Aside from any potential bad apples in the bunch, I had to be so careful and diligent to be sure a neighbor or a relative didn't stumble across my cam page. All that was a small part of the process; there were other surprising dynamics at work in the ongoing back-and-forth of camming.

My first epiphany was that the online interaction wasn't primarily about sex. Often, it wasn't about sex at all. My regulars formed an attachment that was closer to a companionship than a sex partner. Honestly, after you've seen a naked woman diddling herself with her expensive dildo, how much is left to reveal or titillate? Plus, the guys could never touch me.

So there had to be something else, something beyond the superficial physical appeal that any cam customer could get by renting porn on pay-per-view. I learned that men came back day after day simply because I would listen. Or, more precisely, I heard them. Most were looking for a meaningful connection. They were a lot like me in that regard.

We're a lonely society. That isolation is often made worse by a digital world that was, ironically, created to connect us. I'm Miss Mega-introvert myself, but even I understand the primal longing to bond with someone who actually gives a shit. That is so essentially human. My cam clients craved what we all want: reassurance that we are not alone. Love. Friendship. Those interactions were not one-way streets. My public chat space was a strange, diverse melting pot. Guys from twenty to fifty.

Lawyers, programmers, truck drivers, athletes, landscapers, and unemployed men traded comments and the kind of banter you'd hear in a sports bar. They became friends with each other and with me. It was a close-knit community where they felt welcomed, a safe space for everyone.

Any guy who logged onto my account knew that there was zero chance of rejection. He didn't have to be nervous about talking to me. We were going to get to know each other, we were going to laugh and enjoy ourselves, and it was all going to be a positive experience. That is what kept my regulars coming back, sometimes logging on every single day.

Another big insight? Camming held many of the same benefits for me. Even though I would never enjoy the physical part of camming, quite the opposite was true of the social interaction. At times, I felt like it was my therapy. I could be honest about almost everything in my life. Just as I would always welcome any guy on my page, the regulars never judged me. They listened and they cared. Chat with someone for days, months, and years, and you learn about his family, job, friends, and every aspect of his life. It was an entirely honest and forthright exchange except for one lie: I was always single to my cam regulars. Owning up to even a casual dating relationship would have cost me money.

Off camera, I wrestled with conflicting emotions. I didn't have any moral problems with what I was doing. I saw camming in simple, stark terms. It was a matter of survival and the only way I had found to get out of a bleak existence. That didn't mean I never felt ashamed. I did.

I can't imagine any reasonable person who wouldn't feel at least some shame at getting naked for complete strangers in exchange for money. I also had a lot of guilt over what my newfound profession did to Bobby. It had to be so emasculating. His wife got naked in front of strangers and he lived off the windfall. I could tell myself that it was all to create a better life for the three of us, but I knew full well that wasn't the truth. Bobby wasn't a part of whatever vague long-term plans I had. I also understood that I was tearing a piece of his heart out.

That I was willing to do such an awful thing to him was a sign of just how much I hated poverty. Some life decisions have both tremendously good and awfully bad consequences. You try to figure out how to make your peace with what you choose to do. I wasn't so naïve to think that once I started camming I could just stop and walk away. You can't unring that digital bell. Nothing on the Internet ever goes away. Poverty and how we were living were so ugly to me that I gladly made that bargain and accepted all that came with it. Unfortunately, Bobby was forced to accept it as well.

As the money came in and I showed no signs of slowing down, he gave in to the inevitable. He stopped trying to sad-face me into quitting. He took a new tack. If he couldn't sway me with his pain, he would support me so completely that it would be obvious I couldn't do without him. It was in his nature because he was a supportive, good person. The plan was reasonable even if it was doomed to fail. There was a small upside for him in any case. As I became the breadwinner, the pressure was off him to get and keep a regular job. Both of us enjoyed a much better life.

We could afford the townhouse for the first time since we moved in. I filled the kitchen with our favorite foods. Not healthy, but more indulgent than we had ever been able to afford.

I saved enough money after the first month of camming to buy something I had wanted since I had lost all my pregnancy weight: new boobs. Let me tell you, lose sixty pounds in a hurry right after having a baby and it takes a toll on the old girlish figure. That was most glaringly obvious with my breasts. They were prematurely saggy and the feature I was most self-conscious about on camera. Camming gave me both the money and a "business" excuse to get them done. I visited a plastic surgeon the Frenemy referred me to. As part of the process, the nurse had me try on different sizers.

"I'm not sure how large I should go. How do I pick a size?"

She smiled at me, like she was my older sister giving me heartfelt advice. "Nobody is ever disappointed by going larger." Okay then. Double Ds it was.

It was a ridiculous choice. I'm five feet, three inches tall on a good day. Hang double-D cups off my frame and it turned me into a pair of boobs with legs. I was too inexperienced to understand that, and it would take me a while to see that I had to reduce them. In the moment, though, I couldn't have been happier. I flew through the surgery and came home to a husband who had bought me a Dairy Queen ice cream cake to celebrate. I recovered by lounging in bed eating piece after piece (and throwing them up after I did), and binge-watching five seasons of *Dexter*. Four days later, I was back up on my cam.

My new chest was the exact opposite of my post-weight loss

grandma tits. Although my regulars would always advise me against making any physical change I was contemplating, the reaction to my new assets once I went live was always universal approval. Call it superficial if you want, the change gave me more confidence, and made me happier. I felt like I was creating a better me, although I wasn't totally aware that I was also creating a whole different woman.

Camming became more and more lucrative as earning turned into a sort of ongoing contest I had with myself. Like a video gamer playing hour after hour trying for a new high score, I went online religiously to rack up the figures in my cam-site payment account. Theoretically, I could still make zero dollars in any given session, but that never happened. I was becoming skilled at connecting with my clients and was handsomely rewarded for that ability.

I was less adept at managing all the money that came in. Instead of saving, I spent my newfound wealth. I was looking to get far away from any sign of poverty. The first order of business was ditching that Dodge Neon.

I traded it in for a brand-new midnight-black Hyundai Elantra. I paid extra for every option they offered. I wanted to park my new ride in front of a crib that would show off my success, so I moved the three of us to an outrageously bougie townhouse on the lake. It was completely over the top, the fanciest home I'd ever been in. The two-story stunner sat on a huge piece of property and even had its own dock. The master bedroom was connected to a luxurious marble spa bathroom with a walk-in shower and a two-person tub.

I was banking money, taking care of my daughter, and

making progress. I wasn't standing in line at the food bank and felt confident that I never would again. My life was moving in exactly the right direction, with one exception—my marriage. Splitting up with Bobby had always been part of the plan, but now it gained an urgency because I saw my marriage as the sole remaining speed bump in my road forward. Problem was, I had an ingrained people-pleasing tendency and a fierce aversion to confrontation. Sitting Bobby down and telling him it was over was an incredibly hard thing for me to do. I put it off as long as I could. Finally, though, I realized the only fair thing to do was just yank off the bandage.

I told him that he had to move out, that our marriage was over and that I wasn't going to support him any longer. I bought him a secondhand Toyota and he piled what he could fit into the car and drove off. I had set him adrift and he was lost. He bounced around for a few weeks sleeping in his car. Finally, he came up with a plan to rebuild. We agreed that I would pay for a training course that would prep him to work in the growing Canadian oil industry. It meant he would have to move to another province for the short term. It was an incredible sacrifice to make, both us of knowing he'd miss Izzy terribly, but it would give him his own path forward.

I think Bobby also needed some physical separation from me, to process his feelings at what surely must have felt like a heartless betrayal. I could hardly blame him. I had known the cruelty of abandonment and would forever harbor guilt for visiting that soul-crushing pain on him. He drove off and we were now separated in every way possible.

I had mixed emotions as a newly single mom. I was ashamed of how I had treated my husband, but I was thrilled to be earning good money and forging a life free of poverty. It felt so good to be in control. I had the world's most beautiful daughter, the brightest future I had ever known, and what looked to be a long-term career. The only thing I was lacking was a loving romantic relationship. That would prove more elusive than all the rest.

Camming is a little like being a cop or a nurse in that you tend to socialize with other people who understand the unique experience of your work life. In the months after Bobby moved out, The Frenemy was just about my only social contact. We put up with each other because there wasn't anyone else. We both needed someone who understood, someone to hang out with and blow off a little steam. Saturday night would roll around, we'd grab a vodka-cranberry or three, catch a local cover band, and check out the bar traffic.

Over time, though, other cam girls messaged me. It was nice to get a random, "Hey, how are ya?" text. I got to know those women from afar as we bonded over shared stories of guys who liked to see woman do bizarre things with produce, or men who had obvious mommy issues. All those anecdotes we couldn't share with friends and families. It was nice to connect, but I didn't really mind the secrecy and isolation of camming. I'm a flaming introvert. I'm good on my own, just sweet Izzy and me.

Plus, I was getting a lot of socializing and exposure camming. It did more than just pay the rent and keep the lights on. It was a shot in the arm for my self-esteem and confidence, neither of which had ever been particularly healthy. My cam account evolved into something about much more than physical pleasure. My regulars didn't come back day after day because they were so intrigued by my boobs. See them once, they don't change. No, they showed up like clockwork for something much more elusive than masturbation inspiration. They logged on for pain-free social interaction and mutual support.

It's the easiest thing in the world to judge other people, and sex workers are an obvious, appealing target for people just aching to look down their noses at someone. That's never made sense to me. As a cam girl, I worked a legal job. I paid taxes and supported my daughter. I did nothing on camera that many, many wives and girlfriends don't do for their husbands, boyfriends, or girlfriends. I wasn't hurting anybody and was, in fact, providing a valuable service to my customers.

My guys knew that. It was one of the reasons they gave me universally positive feedback, and I gave them a connection most of them lacked in their day-to-day lives. They could have bought an adult DVD if that's all there was to it. I connected with those guys, the ones who came back again and again. Call it a form of friendship. Before you laugh at that idea, stop and think about how many of your Facebook friends you've actually talked to in, like, the last three months.

I hadn't had a reason to be proud of much in my life, but I was proud that I was making a living on my own effort and initiative. I was proud that nobody was helping me. I was standing on my own two feet, carving out a good life for Izzy and me. Of course,

I didn't mind one bit that as Jessica Wilde evolved, she looked less and less like the old me, that insecure fat chick that I was only too happy to shed. I saw Jessica as a big improvement.

Jessica and camming. That powerhouse duo meant I had disposable income and the free time to spend it. It was a cool blast of happiness to really discover that there was lots of life to be lived beyond pure survival mode. I dared open up to the possibility of having fun for fun's sake, like the twenty-two-year-old I was. A little something something beyond working and being a mommy.

When the cam site management invited all the cam girls to Las Vegas to sign photos in the company's booth at the AVN Adult Entertainment Expo, I thought, "Hell yes. Sin city, why not?" AVN is a porn convention, but the happening was also a chance to meet other cam girls in person, make new friends, get up to some harmless shenanigans, and rack up a little business exposure. I had never been to America, much less the playground that I imagined Las Vegas to be. All in all, the convention looked like a gift-wrapped chance to enjoy the hell out of myself.

Bobby had returned to Kelowna and landed a good job. We had set up a visitation schedule and a routine. Like the good man he was, Bobby picked up the childcare slack whenever I needed to travel for work or pleasure. I dropped Izzy off with him and headed to Kelowna International Airport. I shared the flight with The Frenemy.

We hadn't become much closer. We'd always be a little too competitive and different personalities to have a real friendship. Still, we were the only people in each other's local orbit who understood what we did for a living. We talked a little but spent most of the flight and taxi ride from McCarren International Airport in shared silence.

I looked out the window as a dreary landscape of lookalike stucco houses and lackluster, treeless streets scrolled by. I was surprised how bland everything was. My entire impression of Las Vegas had been formed by scenes out of movies like *Casino* and *Ocean's Eleven*. The only photos I'd ever seen of the city were of The Strip, all those casinos lit up in a million shades of neon. It was a shock to realize the real Las Vegas was mile after mile of faceless suburbs where people went about ordinary lives. I could relate; the city itself had identity issues. The Strip, though, did not disappoint. It was quite obviously the heart and soul of that town, and one hell of a scene.

We stayed at the Hard Rock Hotel and Casino, where the convention was being held. I dropped my bags off in my room and headed downstairs to check out the convention scene. The vibe was electric. There was a lot of hustle, the buzz of business being done. A sea of happy fans crowded the convention floor full of all kinds of expectation and lust. I swung by the cam site booth and met a group of other cam girls that I knew only through Twitter text messages. They were solid gals who were incredibly welcoming, like I was one of their tribe.

The porn performers, on the other hand, quite obviously looked down on us. I found that ironic and downright hysterical. I thought, "What could they be on about?" I controlled my work environment. I wasn't at the mercy of sleazy, disreputable producers trying to force me to do increasingly degrading things.

A girl on set with a cameraman, director, and gaffers? She did what they said or she looked for somewhere else to earn a payday. Some guy on the other side of my cam got out of line? Bam. I shut him down and blocked the living bejesus out of him. I even made better money than many porn stars. I controlled who saw me at work, and what they saw. I had complete power. That was a lot more than any porn star could say.

The fans didn't make a distinction between the two. Like every other booth at AVN, ours had a long line all day. I took group selfies and posed for photos with the excited young men who wanted to document their time among the hotties. It was exhilarating, but I kept my eyes on the prize. Fun was all part of the package, but I was on the lookout for business with a capital B. I gave out my cam information to the guys who came by the booth and kept my antenna up for any other legitimate prospects. Sure enough, ten minutes before I took my first break, a golden opportunity came knocking. A corporate type in his mid-forties, wearing a chic, pricey suit and tie, introduced himself and handed me his business card with the *Playboy* bunny logo on it.

"I think you have the kind of look that we're after. Give me a call after you get home and we'll talk about some ways to get you in the door."

It wasn't an offer for a centerfold spread, but it was a helluva starting point.

"I will, thanks."

*Playboy* was tasteful modeling, a huge platform, and a step up from camming. The magazine had launched a lot of acting careers and opened heavy doors for women like me. That business card was the cherry on a sundae that was my exciting first day in Las Vegas. As traffic at the booth wound down, I joined my rowdy sorority of camming sisters and we headed out for some greasy happy hour snacks, stiff drinks, and mad chatter. We exchanged outrageous stories of the things we'd seen and heard from the pros at the other booths, had a ton of laughs, and cemented friendships that would last far beyond the convention. I didn't fully realize it, but I was building a support network with sisters from another mister who understood what it was like managing a persona created just for a tiny electronic eyeball on top of a computer screen.

I came to Las Vegas fully expecting to run into some reptiles. After all, you don't dive into the ocean and be surprised to get wet. We didn't have to wait long for the night crawlers to find us. The Frenemy and I got invited out for a late night of clubbing with the rap group Three 6 Mafia. It seemed like just about the perfect Vegas adventure.

The night started out like some surreal music video scene, with us rolling up to the Millionaires Club in the back of a Rolls-Royce Phantom. We stepped out into the electric night with blunt smoke swirling all around us. We waltzed right past the velvet rope into the pulsing club, all the guys heavy in gold bling. The rappers' style, the club, the people, all seemed right in step with the decadence on display up and down The Strip. I felt like I was playing dress-up and celebrity for a night, and I had a blast until the evening took a left turn. A guy on the fringe of the group's entourage informed me that I would be sleeping with anybody who wanted me to, starting with him. That was to be the price of hanging out and drinking on the group's bottle-service tab. I couldn't stop myself from laughing in his face.

"What you think's so funny?"

"I'm not going to do that. Not in a million years."

"Why not?"

"I'm not going to fuck someone for champagne and a seat in a VIP booth."

"No? Then you're just a waste of good pussy."

With that, I started laughing again and headed to the exit. I grabbed a taxi and went back to my room at the Hard Rock. I nested down for a night wrapped in the luxury of my super soft queen-size bed, watching *Iron Man* on pay-per-view, and scarfing microwave popcorn by the fistful. As far as I knew, The Frenemy stayed out all night with the rappers. We never discussed what she was asked to do, or how she handled those demands. I didn't want to know.

I met another Vegas lizard in the hotel bar the next night. Max was a handsome, well-built guy with the overly manicured four-day almost beard of a sports-show ex-jock commentator. He was the type of guy who spent far too much time on personal grooming and admiring himself in the mirror. I was still young, a little naïve, and maybe a bit reckless. Just the same, I wasn't stupid. I sized up that joker's full measure right off. As we talked, Max couldn't help himself from checking out every hot female that bounced by. He told me he was a mover and shaker in public relations and event hosting. That tracked. He seemed like the type to spin stories and collect women, a bullshitter that would appeal to a certain type of entrepreneur looking to do business in Vegas and be treated like a VIP in the process. Within the first ten minutes, Max insinuated that he had been a special forces badass. I suspected that the truth was less glamorous.

He was transparent, but I had already learned from my time at the women's shelter that anyone—regardless of character defects—is capable of giving you valuable insights if you're willing to listen and do a little reading between the lines. As predictable as he might have been, Max gave me a gift that night. When the conversation turned to business books, he mentioned *The Purple Cow*, by Seth Godin, along with a couple of other social-media marketing books. Godin's book turned out to be an eye-opener for me, full of valuable insight on building a business and a brand. It nurtured my obsession with social media marketing, business development, and self-improvement books. It was a lot of food for thought to go with a couple of free White Russians. Not a bad night, all in all.

As interesting, fun, and enlightening as the trip turned out to be, I was incredibly happy to get home. It felt good to roll through my sleepy town, and slide under my own fluffy down comforter, with my wonderful Izzy asleep in her room. Unfortunately, I didn't realize that there would be some unexpected and unpleasant fallout from the trip.

The bigger the secret you have in life, the harder it is to keep. As discreet and careful as I had been around my family, they found out about my career in the most bizarre and random way. My mother was watching one of her daytime talk shows, and there was a special segment on the AVN convention for some reason. As bad luck would have it, the B-roll footage that ran in the background during the segment included the cam site booth with you-know-who standing center frame. I hadn't unpacked my bags when my cousin texted me: "Are you really a cam girl?" I stood there staring at that text, a little jet-lagged and thinking, "What to the what now?"

Fortunately, my family wasn't much interested in my life. That included something juicy like the reveal that I was, in fact, Jessica Wilde. It didn't even move the needle for them, and most of my relatives never brought it up to me or asked any questions. Even my mom barely mentioned it. I think the idea of the reality behind what I did for a living and what discussing it might entail held little appeal for her. We had never been good at opening up and being entirely honest and forthright with one another, and camming would have been a minefield topic of conversation.

It wouldn't have been a big deal if everyone had made a fuss. The only opinion that mattered to me out of the whole lot was my grandmother's. She was a devout Catholic, and I was worried that she would think I was hellbound and refuse to have anything to do with me once she found out what I did for a living.

I couldn't bear that thought; of all the rejections I'd gone through in life, that would have been the absolute worst. I realized that I had to suck it up and face the music. I got in my car and made the long anxious drive to her house to sit down for a face-to-face chat. As it turned out, I was foolish to have worried. She was the most reasonable, loving, and accepting person I knew. I sat down across from her at her kitchen table. I looked into her kind brown eyes and her wrinkly face, and I told her straight out what I was doing and why. I explained how I had gotten started, and—without going into details—what camming did and didn't entail. She wasn't thrown for a loop. This woman had lived through a world war, the Vietnam era, and the sixties. I'm sure there wasn't much she hadn't seen. She nodded and took a beat thinking it over. "Well, you're not hurting anyone and at least you're not a prostitute. I don't see what all the fuss is about."

It was a wonderful moment for me, a little bit of sugar from the most supportive person in my life. It was such a commonsense way to look at things. It really made me think about all the people I'd come across in my life who were so intent on judging others just to avoid dealing with their own warts and clay feet.

There are a heck of a lot of insecure and hypocritical folks out there in the world. They don't know themselves, or don't like who they see in the mirror. If they can find someone they can feel superior to, they don't have to worry about their own flaws, about the person they see in the mirror each morning. It's sad, but a lot of the world has that sickness. I knew there was nothing wrong with what I was doing, but I continued to keep it secret to avoid dealing with small-minded people and petty judgments. Over time, that would change. More and more people—old high school acquaintances, people I had known growing up—would find out. Within a few years, I would stop caring what anyone thought and embrace the fact that I wasn't ashamed of what I had done or would do for a living. I was actually proud to be a successful, self-employed businessperson.

In the meantime, I appreciated the doors that Jessica Wilde was opening. I had that business card from the *Playboy* exec and it inspired me to edit and improve her. I had the flat, undefined tummy of someone who had lost a lot of weight but not gotten toned. I hadn't yet discovered the wonders of the gym, so I decided to have a tummy tuck in case my brush with *Playboy* turned into an actual photo shoot. It was my second surgical improvement but would not be my last.

That there was even the remote possibility of appearing in *Playboy* made me dream about a bigger future than I had ever dared consider. I felt like nothing was off the table. Maybe I could have a mainstream modeling career, or even find a role on TV or in a movie. I was well beyond pure survival now, and Jessica Wilde had gotten me there. Ultimately, the guy from *Playboy* took a little air out of my balloon when I called him and he offered me a position as a server and sometimes hostess at the Playboy mansion, making just above minimum wage. He had never intended to put me in the magazine. It was a small speed bump. I knew bigger things were out there if I was willing to go get them, work hard, and be smart.

Among those bigger things was the personal brass ring of true love. I was earning a good living just a few years after sleeping on a cot in a women's shelter. I had gotten through that, turned my life around and made things happen. A truly loving relationship? It didn't seem harder to achieve than anything I'd already done.

I thought I was worthy of a family with a partner who supported me as I supported him, someone I could trust to accept me for who I was—even as I was making the strange and unpredictable transition to Jessica Wilde. Really, it seemed so simple, genuine love. Be loved and love in return. I never stopped to consider the trail of broken, dysfunctional relationships behind all the people I knew. I was me. I had a right to dream. True love didn't seem like the impossible goal it once had. In fact, it seemed totally reasonable.

With no in-person social network to speak of, I went back to Plenty of Fish in my search for Mr. Right. I quickly landed on the profile of a guy named Tyler. The man checked all the boxes. He was five years older than I was and already had two kids. He was a web developer who, from the looks of it, had his life thoroughly together. More pretty than handsome, Tyler was way better looking than any guy I had ever dated. He was six feet tall, with the athletic build of the avid amateur hockey player that he was. His shaggy blonde hair and crooked smile gave him an appealingly boyish look.

Tyler would be the first guy I actually chose, rather than having no options beyond saying yes or no to the rare mope who asked me out. It was a new experience and a Jessica Wilde moment. I wasn't the minimum-wage overweight girl who couldn't stand looking in the mirror or stepping onto the scale. The one who had to say, "Yes," because so few guys asked. I was Jessica now, wasn't I? Big boobs, nice crib, new tummy tuck. A sparkling brand-new me. That Tyler was good-looking with a solid job and ready-made family—a "catch" by any yardstick—made him a challenge, a test I set for Jessica Wilde.

I shot him a message. He got right back to me. That night, we messaged back and forth. He was a funny guy, far from full of himself. We agreed to a first date. There was an EDM concert at an arena about four hours from Kelowna. We drove the lengthy trip together, talking and joking like we had known each other for a long time. He was an easy person to hang out with and the drive flew by.

We got separate hotel rooms and had an absolute blast at the concert. On the drive back home, I told him what I did for a living and held my breath. This was the acid test. If he was going run the other way, best he do it early rather than later. It would be okay either way. I wouldn't respect a guy who had a problem with how I made my money. Tyler said all the right things and didn't seem bothered in the least.

We were incredibly compatible. Inside a couple months, we had met each other's kids and I had gotten to know and like Tyler's family. It all went so smoothly that I didn't even think about the fact that we were moving at light speed. Everything was headed in the right direction. One night as we were sitting at his dining room table having just finished dinner, Tyler said, "Why don't we find a place together?"

I was that perfect storm of young, naïve, and impatient. It had been three whole months. What were we waiting for? I'd seen the Hallmark movies; this was the next step into happily ever after. I didn't so much as hesitate, before saying "That would be great." It would be great. I had never known true love, but I assumed this was it. It certainly had all the trappings. We had kids, good-paying jobs, nice cars. Wasn't moving in together the logical next step? The thing people did? Why wait? I had my Prince Charming, now I wanted my palace. The sad truth that I could never have possibly admitted to myself was that I wouldn't have known true love if it bit me on the butt.

Tyler and I were both doing well financially, enough so that we could afford to shop at the high end of Kelowna's rental market. As I had climbed out of poverty, my living space had taken on an oversized importance in my mind. Not only did I want a place where I could hunker down and nurture my inner introvert, I also worked at home. Much more than that, though, my home was about maintaining control and emotional stability. A nice home kept me feeling grounded and made me happy. It was a tangible symbol of having beaten poverty. In my mind, the house Tyler and I found together was proof positive of how strong the relationship was. There was no room for scrimping. Both of us were already paying sizable rents. Combine those payments into one and, whammo, we qualified for Kardashian-style lodgings.

Our real estate agent was only too happy to oblige these young kids with more money than sense. She found us a five-bedroom McMansion in the foothills outside Kelowna. It was painted white with red trim, and made me think of a wrapped Christmas present. The entryway was right out of a movie, with a twenty-foot vaulted ceiling, white marble floor, and a classic chandelier. There were incredible forested views from every room in the house. The opulent master bath was bigger than the apartment I had moved into from the women's shelter. The bathroom had a two-person jetted whirlpool tub next to a tiled walk-in shower. It was three thousand square feet of sick luxury. We signed the lease the day we saw it.

Even looking backward, I can't figure out what exactly I expected to happen at that point. How everything was supposed to work out. I had never seen a healthy, loving relationship up close, so I had a distorted fairy-tale view of what one looked like in action. I was clueless about the hard work and compromise that goes into any deep, lasting romantic partnership.

Without realizing it, I was trying to live two contradicting lives. Yeah, I wanted the Hallmark postcard family and loving partner I had never experienced. That other me, though, the young woman who got married as a teenager and had a child a year later? She had yet to run. She wanted to have reckless, youthful fun, be appropriately irresponsible, and enjoy the life she was suddenly free to live thanks to Jessica Wilde's hard work. It was a fundamental conflict that I didn't have the awareness to recognize, much less the tools to resolve.

That contradiction made itself known in real ways. I struggled to form any kind of bond with Tyler's seven-year-old Ben and four-year-old Amy. Hidden deep down in a black tar corner of my soul—that place no sane person wants to look—lurked the horrible truth that I resented his kids for taking Tyler's attention off of me. I also had my own daughter to care for and she came first as far as I was concerned. The bigger issue, as it always would be with the men in my life—the one that would ultimately put a .50 caliber bullet through the heart of our relationship—was camming. Jessica Wilde wasn't going to be tamed. No way. When Tyler realized that, he resented the hell out of her.

Sure, he had paid lip service to how okay he was with my profession. Unfortunately, living with the reality of Jessica doing her thing behind a closed door right upstairs was a different story. Inside two weeks, Tyler began grumbling that I should "find a new job." It was predictable I suppose. He met me, liked me, and knew that I was Jessica Wilde. She was this fantasy that any guy could see on his arm and laying in his bed. Then, once the guy became more invested in me—let's call it crossing the line of love—it felt too much like sharing me with other men. Suddenly, camming was cheating and Jessica Wilde was a problem. But she sure as hell wasn't a problem for me. For me, she had been the big solution and nothing short of a life-changing gold mine.

Tyler grew distant and moody. He started channeling his inner jerk, being rude and dismissive. He didn't want to go out to see a band or grab a couple of drinks, and he didn't want to have his family or friends over. I came downstairs one afternoon when he was supposed to be hard at work on a web development project, and found him cruising other girls on Facebook. It was like he was getting payback.

It became clear that there was nothing I could say that would make him happy. The one thing he wanted—the death of Jessica Wilde—was the one thing I wasn't going to give him. Finally, I'd had enough of the snide comments and the increasingly apparent wall he was bricking up between us. It was time for me to move out. Maybe if I put a little distance between us, we could think through everything in our respective bubbles. He might come to his senses. We could get back to where we started.

I found my dream apartment on a local real estate company's website. It was a loft for rent in a building called The Madison, the fanciest address in Kelowna. That was saying something, because the town was quickly gentrifying and there were a lot of nice buildings popping up or being renovated. The apartment was ultra-modern, with floor to ceiling windows, an open floor plan, chef's kitchen, beefy pillars, and gleaming ebonized wood floors. It was just about as super lux as could be, and I absolutely fell in love with it. That night, I sat down with Tyler and told him we needed to have a talk.

"I found a great apartment downtown and I'm moving out."

"What? Why?"

That question threw me. I thought he'd be relieved. Couldn't he see how bad things were?

"This, us, it's not working, Ty. You're angry all the time. You know you are. You don't even want to be in the same room with me, you hate my job so much. I'm not going to stop camming. I told you that. It's how I make a living."

"I know that. I know. Look, I've got a lot on my mind. I'm still getting used to what you do. I mean, it's right here in the house. It's other stuff too. I'm freaked out about my mom. The kids. It's everything, not just you. Don't leave. Stay. Let's work it out. We can get through this."

He was so earnest that I bought it hook, line, and sinker. His mom was fighting advanced stomach cancer. That alone would be enough to wipe any son out. Having three kids to take care of was an understandable reason not to go out as often as we had at the beginning.

Everything he was saying made sense, and I still wanted a happy loving family if I could get it. Maybe that's what normal families struggled with, I thought, stressful times you just had to get through. I badly wanted to believe we could work it out. I agreed to stay and called the real estate agent to tell her I wouldn't be taking the apartment.

Two weeks later, Tyler flipped the script one morning as I was polishing off my breakfast bowl of cornflakes.

"I'm moving out."

I was stunned. "What are you talking about? You said you wanted me to stay, to work it out."

"I know. I was wrong. I can't do it anymore, Jess. I just can't."

I wasn't sure what "it" was. Camming? Life? A relationship? I was devastated. He was really screwing me over. I had given up a dream apartment to "make it work," and less than a month later he just walked into our kitchen and dropped a stick of dynamite into the middle of everything. I felt like a fool for having believed him when he said he wanted me to stay. Now he was going to be just one more person who abandoned me.

He moved out three days later. It hurt so deeply that I couldn't do much more than stand in the middle of the kitchen crying as his family carried boxes out of the house and into the moving van. They avoided looking at me and it was an awkward few hours for all of us. Tyler was all business, though, and he didn't even acknowledge I was there. He managed to pack up and leave without saying a word to me. He couldn't drive away fast enough.

I retreated into my two most reliable stress standbys: TV and bulimia. I gorged on Chinese food and frozen yogurt, purging as soon as I was full. In between, I binge-watched *Modern Family* and tried not to think about Tyler. I got it together to jump on my cam for an hour or two each day because, in camming, you only have to be missing in action for a few days and you can say goodbye to your regulars. I might be crying all morning and feeling like I had been run over by a truck, but when it came time to jump on camera I put on my makeup, channeled Jessica, and showed a happy, sexy face to my clients. I was a hot mess, but I couldn't show it professionally.

Tyler called a week later to tell me his mom had died. As raw as my wound was, as terrible as I felt, he sounded worse. Despite his betrayal, I still had feelings for him. I had never processed the kind of loss that he was dealing with, and I could only imagine how painful it must have been. He asked if I would come to the funeral and I told him I would. I wanted to support him, but I was also desperate to cling to whatever remained of the relationship. If I could have any shot at happiness, it was better than dealing with the pain. The gut-wrenching feeling of being discarded was so overwhelming that I was willing to go to great lengths to avoid or ease that particular agony.

Tyler was openly grateful that I showed up at the funeral. We started dating again. The lease ran out on the house we had shared and I found a beautiful condo to rent two blocks down the street from The Madison. Tyler had landed in a crummy little two-bedroom apartment where he was still living out of boxes and struggling to deal with his mom's death. Even though I still felt stung and gun shy, I held some hope that we could salvage the relationship and get back to a better place.

Then, one night after we had just had sex, Tyler blurted out that he had recently slept with a woman that he had crushed on since middle school. It sounded perversely almost like a boast. I thought, "What the fuck?" It was the no-doubt final nail in the coffin of whatever it was we had or might have had. I got my ass up out of that bed, put on my clothes, and left his apartment. That would be the last time I'd talk to him and certainly the last time I'd ever feel bad about our broken relationship.

I have no idea what possessed Tyler. It was a horrible, classless thing to do, but it was also a small kindness. From the moment I shut the door of his sad little apartment behind me, I no longer felt hurt or abandoned. Whatever feelings I had held for the guy were good and completely squashed. I realized that, in losing him, I had lost nothing.

The experience had wrung me out, though. I badly needed a time-out from work, men, and adulthood. As luck would have it, the Frenemy had introduced me to a spirited, irresponsible young woman named Sarah. She was a leggy redhead with a pair of the biggest boobs I'd ever seen. She made her living as a nude model, and had even posed for *Playboy*. She might not have been someone I would have confided my deepest, darkest secrets to, but the girl was definitely up for just about any kind of hijinks. I figured she'd make a good short-term partner in crime.

We decided to take a three-day break at the Shambhala Music Festival. Shambhala is Canada's version of Burning Man, an incredibly fun, outdoor, four-day music extravaganza held in the gorgeous mountains of Nelson, British Columbia. I rented us the smallest Winnebago I could find, left Izzy with Bobby, and hit the road for our mini adventure.

Shambhala is a wild hippy experience. Sarah and I brought LSD, the drug of choice for that scene. People who have never done acid think it just produces physical hallucinations, that it's only about the bizarre, about hearing colors and seeing music. Sensory distortions are much of the allure, but for me the more powerful effect is the occasional radical change in perspective that LSD creates. Users in the sixties knew that the drug, taken in a safe place with the right people and at a smart dosage, could clarify a mental point of view. A lot of people who drop acid experience life revelations. That's exactly what happened to me.

On the second day of the festival, I had taken a couple more hits than I usually did and the dose had incapacitated me. That wasn't a problem; I just had to sit on the grass by myself until I came down to a more reasonable level. A group of shirtless, long-haired hippie guys were playing frisbee next to me. At one point, the frisbee flew off target and bonked me right in the head. It made a loud, organic sound inside my skull, and I wasn't entirely sure what had happened. I wasn't hurt or angry, just puzzled. The old hard drive wasn't spinning at the usual speed. The guy who threw the frisbee ran over and kneeled down next to me.

"Oh, man, I'm so sorry. Are you okay? We didn't mean to hit you. It was an accident."

I couldn't respond. I was too high to even talk. He looked at my eyes and I suspect he understood exactly what I was going through. He gave me a big hug and said, "You're okay. You'll be fine. You're safe." Then he let me go, patted my shoulder, smiled at me, and retrieved his frisbee.

It struck me as an amazingly kind and compassionate gesture.

Like a flash, it hit me. That basic human interaction, caring for someone, how we treat each other, was the absolute most important thing in life. I felt like I had been avoiding that reality to a certain degree. Instead, I had been putting material goods up on a pedestal. I had been chasing the next shiny purchase, the next thing I could buy to prove I was no longer poor.

It had been that way ever since I had started camming and bringing in good money. The idea that people caring for other people mattered more than anything else was so fundamental, so clear, that I was shocked I had missed it. It wasn't about what kind of car I owned or what brand of purse was hanging off my shoulder, or even what people thought of me. It wasn't about any of that. It was about being a good person, being decent to other people, and showing compassion. That was the most important thing I would ever do.

That realization stuck with me as I came down. It kept popping into my mind as I drove the RV back home after the third day of the festival. I had a new goal. I wanted to be a good, kind, compassionate person. I also wanted to commemorate what I saw as a breakthrough epiphany, a turning point. I turned to my preferred way of acknowledging things to myself—a tattoo. Or, to be more precise, a whole damn sleeve of them. Given the surrealistic, drug-induced way I had gotten to my life-altering realization, it seemed only fitting that the tattoo's theme be Alice in Wonderland.

Tattoos, for those of us who embrace body art, are an integral part of personal identity. They are markers of where you were at a certain stage, place, and time in life. My first tattoo was as frivolous as any ink picked out by a thirteen-year-old would be. Each one I had gotten after that, though, had commemorated something important in my life, from Izzy's birth, to putting Jessica Wilde on camera for the first time. My tats are a roadmap of my experience.

They are also a commitment. Not only does ink stay with you, just getting a tattoo is an ordeal. My sleeve took three separate visits of nine-hours each. The buzz of the needle can make you a little crazy and the pain is no small thing. It's a sacrifice for something that defines personal history and subtly changes or defines who you are. The tattoos I added once I started camming clarified who Jessica Wilde was. They also gave her a distinctive appearance that would prove appealing to a huge number of followers. Little did I know that body art would open other doors for the business of Jessica.

Starting with the books that Max from Las Vegas had clued me in on, I had gone on to consume a bookcase full of social media how-to guides and other business books. I realized that camming was only the tip of an online money-making iceberg. Instagram influencers and Twitch streamers were pulling down six- and seven-figure incomes. Twitter personalities were landing book deals off the strength of a post. People were changing the world by what they posted and getting rich in the process.

Camming had been lucrative, but it had never been fun and fulfilling, and I would be happy to leave it behind. The smart business move was to migrate Jessica Wilde to more mainstream social-media sites and let her really run. YouTube seemed as good a place as any to start.

Maintaining a professional YouTube channel is a surprising amount of work. If you want to exploit the site's algorithm, you have to post often and regularly. Daily is best, but you can't really be serious without throwing up a new video several times a week. That's the only way you can ensure that your channel comes up high in searches, and keeps your current subscribers interested. Shooting and editing a video is also a slog for anyone who isn't a professional video editor.

My biggest problem, though? I had no idea what I should film. I knew the clips had to be short and the quality good. I sure as hell couldn't do anything like what I did on cam. Fortunately, YouTube is its own built-in research tool. I watched just about every video on the YouTube celebrity Jenna Marble's channel to get ideas. Marble was an early presence on the site and she had the knack for creating funny, entertaining, and incredibly watchable videos. I checked out some of YouTube's own "how to get started" videos, then jumped in. Even so, I wasn't sure where my channel would take me or how to make money off of it.

As much as I gave it a shot, it quickly became apparent that I wasn't going to be buying a private jet from my YouTube ad dollars. I couldn't attract enough followers fast enough to move the needle. Just the same, it wasn't wasted effort. A month after I started posting, I noticed that *Inked* magazine was subscribing to my channel. Anyone as into tattoos as I was knew *Inked*. It's the voice of the body art industry and I had long been a subscriber. A few weeks later, *Inked*'s art director hit me up through a message on YouTube. He told me that the magazine wanted me to pose for a cover photoshoot.

I was over the moon. It was a dream come true and couldn't be anything but a big boost for Jessica Wilde's business prospects. *Inked*'s readers, market, and community was a club into which I badly wanted to be accepted. I saw the magazine's clout and cachet as an asset for my brand. It was a no-brainer. I called the art director and agreed to the shoot. He scheduled it for the second week in November.

In all the excitement, I forgot to check my calendar. I had already made reservations for a trip to Disneyland to celebrate Izzy's sixth birthday. My heart sank when I realized the conflict. I knew that *Inked* might bag the shoot altogether if I asked them to reschedule, but I didn't have a choice. Izzy came before Jessica Wilde. Her happiness was more important than mine. Still, it was devastating to think I might have to give up the chance to be an *Inked* cover girl. The more I thought about it, the more rescheduling seemed like a way-too-big ask. A cover photoshoot isn't just a matter of the photographer's time. There would be a stylist, lighting person, and assistants involved. Finally, I just bit the bullet, sent the art director an email asking if they could reschedule, and held my breath. He was entirely cool about it and rescheduled for the last week in November. All that worrying was for nothing.

The trip to Disneyland might as well have been a commercial for the place. It was as close to perfect as you could ask for and maybe even a little more exciting, tinged as it was with the anticipation of my first cover shoot. More importantly, Izzy was in heaven. She couldn't stop smiling as we rode through "Ariel's Undersea Adventure." We both screamed bloody murder for our entire trip on the Incredicoaster, and held hands as we watched the fireworks over downtown Disney every night. It was really a tossup which of us had more fun. By the time we got back home, my batteries were fully recharged and I was ready for my moment of fame. I got on the plane to New York excited for a new chapter in the Jessica Wilde saga.

I landed to a chilly reception in more ways than one. The late fall wind was bitterly cold and cut right through me as I made my way out of JFK arrivals and tried to find the taxi stand. I asked a woman wearing a safety vest where I could grab a taxi.

"Does it look like I fucking work here?"

Okay then. Welcome to New York, Jessica.

*Inked* had booked me into a West Village landmark called The Jane Hotel. It was funky and old New York in a musty, haunted sort of way. The kitchen was closed by the time I checked in so I headed out to the nearest corner deli. I reached the checkout with my banana and yogurt in hand, only to realize I hadn't changed my money. I rummaged through my purse. The best I could do was a Canadian twenty-dollar note.

"Is there any way you can take Canadian money?"

The grouchy dude behind the counter looked like he had just woken up on the back end of a bad bender. He gave me a deadpan stare that said I should know better and, for good measure, told me, "Go fuck yourself."

No Jessica, really, welcome to New York.

The city was rolling out the red carpet for me, bringing every rude New Yorker movie scene ever filmed to life. Adding to the general ambience of my trip, I came to believe the hotel really was haunted. Elevator doors popped open and closed of their own accord, there was a mysteriously ominous thumping inside the walls. The ghost of a murder victim seeking revenge? Ancient Native Americans come to reclaim their land? Who knew? Whatever the cause, the Jane was rocking a full-on creepy vibe. I think the management was embracing it, because the place was kind of decorated like the set for a season of *American Horror Story*. Funny enough, though, the room and my bed were mega comfortable, the noises all quieted down after ten, and I got great night's sleep. I came to like the hotel and took it as a good omen.

In the morning, I excitedly got myself together and headed downtown to the photography studio. Manhattan is an easy place to navigate and I found the building without a problem, but there was no directory of offices. I asked the first guy I saw, a rough teamster type moving a large wooden box on a dolly, where the photography studio was. It was clear he, too, had gotten the memo about my visit.

"I don't fucking know. Find the mailboxes."

I thought, "Wow, New Yorkers sure love a hearty F bomb."

Meandering through concrete hallways, I peeked into every open door. I saw celebrities, models, photographers. It was glamour on parade up in this old building. Finally, I came to a heavy door with a piece of paper taped to the front. The paper had "INKED" printed in bold on it. The whole mood of the trip shifted. I pushed the door open and suddenly I was in the center of an amazing hive of activity.

I had never felt more pampered or special. A makeup artist fussed over my face, trying to find a movie star in there somewhere. The wardrobe person held outfit after outfit up in front of me, laying out clothes for me to try on. The photographer was a sweetie who had tons of talent and experience, and a clear vision for the shoot.

She shot image after image, as I struck dozens of poses. I tried to do whatever she said. It wasn't easy because, as with every other photo shoot I'd ever do, I wrestled with Imposter Syndrome. I felt so incredibly awkward, as if I had forgotten what hands were for and what you did with them. Suddenly, I didn't know how normal people moved their legs or how to stand "naturally," or turn my head and smile. It was terrifying, but also exhilarating and, in an odd way, even empowering.

I've learned that personal growth mostly only happens outside your personal comfort zone. Photo shoots have always driven that point home for me. The biggest challenge would always be the feeling that I was a huge fake getting one over on everyone involved. The same unnerving thoughts ran through my head as the camera clicked and klieg lights blazed bright on me: "Who the hell do I think I am wasting this photographer's time? I don't know what I'm doing. Do they not realize that?"

I've come to realize that I'll never get loose of that feeling and maybe that's a good thing, growth-wise. In any case, it doesn't really matter. The unique thrill of becoming different characters on camera, of nailing a photo shoot, is every bit as strong as any mental affliction I might encounter. Each wardrobe change involved a complete redo of my hair and makeup, and created a brand-new woman. It was as much fun as it was intimidating.

Over time and more photo shoots I would develop a way of

coping with Imposter Syndrome and the related anxiety. It came down to this: I understand I'm not alone. I've met a lot of high-functioning, incredibly introverted professionals in my life. Tackling big goals isn't a walk in the park for any of them. Something as simple as speaking in front of a dozen people can be incredibly unnerving. It's easy to imagine the worst. Embarrassment. Harsh judgment. That's a shared human experience. When I start running circles in my own head, I take a mini time-out, breathe and think about how everyone around me is struggling, too.

I come back again and again to the reassuring reality that, for the most part, everyone wants you to succeed. They're rooting for you. Photographers want Jessica to shine so they can capture portfolio-worthy, jaw-dropping images. Makeup artists are aiming to knock the ball out of the park. The lighting guy wants each shot lit perfectly. We're all rowing in the same direction. The audience in front of the introvert on stage? They want to hear what he has to say. It's a stupidly simple thought, but it has helped me get through a lot. In fact, more than that, it has helped me embrace and even enjoy the experience. I realized right after the last photo was taken, as the makeup artist packed up her gear, I was on a high. In fact, I thought, "How can I make this feeling last? I can't be done now. This needs to be the beginning."

I went back to the hotel. I hunkered down in my room with a heady supply of Cheetos, and enjoyed a night of pay-per-view rom-coms. It was the perfect way to decompress after a long day. I flew home early the next morning, never having seen the images from the shoot. It was just how the industry worked. The first time I would lay eyes on those photos, would be when Inked sent me the issue.

When I finally opened my mailbox to find the advance copy, the cover was a Bettie Page-style shot. Not my favorite, but a cool image. Inside, there was a spread of several more photos and they were all stunning. I turned the pages slowly, thinking to myself, "Wow, they look really good." Jessica. She was stunning in every one of those photos. Why wouldn't she? Girl had it going on. I had a hard time squaring those fun and sexy images with the me I saw in the mirror every morning. Which was the truth? The Jessica in those photos had a bright future and was in control. The mirror woman was going to enjoy the fruits of her labor, but wanted something different. The real me had her crosshairs set on a different challenge. I was still holding out for true love.

# -6-

# MY HEART IS IN MY VAGINA

Mosaic Books in downtown Kelowna has a huge magazine rack with about a gazillion magazines on display in tiered rows. It took me a few minutes, but I finally found the issue of *Inked* three rows back, lined up next to the bodybuilding mags. I looked back at me from the cover, fifties hairdo and tats on full technicolor display. It was the third store I'd visited and it would be the third copy I bought. I wanted to keep experiencing that small jolt of excitement from when I first saw the cover. It seems like such a small thing, a magazine cover. Not to me. As a woman with next to no self-esteem, someone who had been practically homeless once and felt like an imposter far too often, it was a huge moment. I was proud, and high on the sheer possibilities that cover represented.

I was never the kind of person who would fuss over a five-year masterplan or detailed business strategy. When it came to business—unlike romance—I trusted myself. If there was something bigger to be built on the start of that magazine cover,

I was confident that the woman in the picture could build it. I wasn't sure what that might be, or if it might be nothing at all. Maybe a tattoo magazine cover would be the highlight of my career and my business life. I suppose that was one option, but I wasn't going to entertain that possibility.

Jessica Wilde was growing up, getting stronger, becoming more successful. She was all about banking the coin. That was the real point behind that chick camping it up on the glossy cover. Come hell or high water I was never going to be poor again, and I damn sure wasn't ever going to let Izzy know poverty.

This much was true, though. If I was finally going to break completely loose of camming and exploit any opportunity that cover represented, I had to build out Jessica's "platform." She needed an audience far larger than the diehard men that showed up every week on a cam feed. I had my sights set on more mainstream modeling and entertainment work. Instagram was the natural first step in that direction.

I had watched closely as Instagram exploded. The photo-focused social media site had launched in 2010 and done well, but it had really exploded when Facebook bought it in 2012. From that point on, it became the preferred site for celebrities, wannabe celebrities, and the new breed of animal called "influencers." It was a way to show off golden lives and sell products, brand mentions, and other stuff.

Who cared if none of that was the truth? Fans gobbled up the fabulous fictions packaged as delicious visual fantasies. They flocked to images of Nicki Minaj posing in her gaudy decadent crib, or Dwayne "The Rock" Johnson's feel-good on-set selfies and muscle porn. It slowly dawned on me that Instagram was custom made for Jessica Wilde ... or vice versa. Meanwhile, fans put up their own accounts, using their iPhone filters and creative photo editing to present shiny new versions of their lives, their friends, their families, and themselves.

Photos were destined to become the drivers of social media. The latest iPhone won't help you write better, but it can make anyone a passably good, if not great, photographer. People who loved to post on Facebook about how wonderful their vacation had been found even more gratification by carefully curating the photos they showed on Instagram of their long weekend at Yosemite. The right photo collage got more "likes" and more attention, and led account holders to work even harder on the digital fictions everyone was crafting about their lives. Even on Twitter, influencers realized the power of sprinkling photos and videos into their tweets. It was all about chasing likes.

The "like" button is the crack of social media. You get five likes on a photo or a post, you want ten on the next one. The key to it all? Our endless pursuit of happiness. The Lovely Lie of social media is that we're chasing happiness in an illusion. We think if we follow someone who makes us laugh, or horny, or cry, that they will make us happy for at least a moment. Then we put up our own posts that are washed and dried to present someone we aren't—an incredibly happy, successful person—in the vain hope that the illusion will create a reality. It's like trying to lose weight on a diet of Big Macs. It feels awfully good for a moment, but only gets us further from actual, real, lasting happiness.

I understood all of that. I knew that those of us who were

trying to make a living in that digital Wild West were even more focused on likes and followers. It was the algorithm at work. You liked one of my posts, and the friends and family who follow you were more likely to see my post and follow me. Every like was a business review for Jessica Wilde, and a chance to chase out the thread and gather more followers. More followers meant more ad dollars or potential business deals. Get it right, and you would find yourself in six- or even seven-figure territory.

Still, I made the leap to Instagram with some reservations. Discretion remained hugely important to me. I didn't want my worlds to collide. Even though I was phasing out my cam work, I feared my Instagram followers would discover my cam channel, or my cam customers might pop up on Instagram and give the game away. Building Jessica's Instagram following had to be a separate thing, not an extension of the camming I was leaving behind. I fretted over it for a time, finally thinking, "Screw it. There's no way I blow up in popular culture or entertainment without taking some risks." I went ahead and set up the Jessica Wilde Instagram account.

It was a slow start. I wasn't sure what to post at first. I didn't have a clear idea of how to play Instagram. What picture or narrative was going to push Jessica Wilde toward a bright and shining future?

I posted a few selfies and felt my way along. Guys started showing up and hitting the "follow" button. Eventually, I'd learn that my followers—and potential followers—wanted every image to be a cover shot. I refined my selfie technique to mirror the professional shoots I had started commissioning on my own, to create content I could use wherever and whenever I wanted. The brand built steadily as I fed the Instagram machine, but it wasn't all sweetness and light.

For all the potential it presented, Instagram created an identity crisis in my life. Jessica Wilde was no longer secret, hidden behind a pay wall. The more I refined her for the Instagram audience, the more she fostered gross misconceptions about my flesh-and-blood reality. People understandably thought she was me. The common assumption—but the one that missed the mark the most—was that I had some kind of dreamy romantic life. Judging by the comments on my posts, a whole lot of people thought I was regularly wooed by millionaires, rap moguls, and movie stars, whisked away in private Gulfstreams while consuming endless bottles of Cristal on my way to exotic ports of call.

Yeah. About that…

I might have been struggling to figure out who I really was, but I knew for damn sure that I was not Instagram Jessica. She was a convenient, profitable, and useful creation. But man, oh man, I wish I could have blocked any potential Mr. Right from laying his peepers on her. Camming, for all the issues it had created in my relationships, was at least a hidden evil. I could block a boyfriend from my cam account. Hell, I could block a whole damn country.

Instagram was a whole lot more exposed. Once a guy saw Jessica, got to know her, the real me paled in comparison. Every man I met on a dating site would inevitably do a search, check out my YouTube channel or Instagram page, and fall for that deceitful vixen. They revered her perfection.

Instagram Jessica rolled out of bed sexy and ready for action. She always looked good on a man's arm, was cool and collected, and had a witty comeback to shoot down would-be suitors that didn't make her high bar. Me? I was a flesh-and-blood girl, with warts and clay feet. I bloated for five days every month. I got up in the morning looking like a normal human being, with morning breath and bed hair.

I wasn't that Instagram goddess. She didn't need anyone. Me? I craved a real connection, to discover and be known, understood in a deeply transparent and personal way. I wanted a man to see and appreciate the me that wasn't Photoshopped, the person who had so much more inside than could ever be captured by a camera lens. The real me wasn't worried about perfection. I wanted to fall hopelessly in love and be hopelessly loved in return. Credit where credit is due, I had the hopeless part right.


I dated a few guys in the year after Tyler, but nothing stuck. The final hurdle for me, that mysterious point when I knew it might be an actual "relationship," was sex. My dates weren't making it that far. Despite the camming and the sultry Instagram photos, it actually took a lot for me to open up sexually to a man. The stars had to align for my panties to come off. I was no fan of one-night stands. That meant the dates I went on after Tyler fizzled because the men had already fallen for the myth of Jessica Wilde. They assumed the first date would end with exactly what Jessica promised—a memorable romp between the sheets.

That wasn't me, though. I was on the lookout for an intangible something … that impossible thing to touch or define that we call "chemistry." If I was going to jump into bed with a man, I usually had to convince myself that a relationship lay right on the other side of an orgasm. When that happened, I would be off to the happily ever after. I could spend the immediate afterglow staring at the dark bedroom ceiling, imagining what the rest of our lives together would be like. If there was chemistry, if the sex worked, I fell. Because my heart is in my vagina, that's why.

Meeting anyone, getting to that magical point where we made it to bed, much less where lovemaking became love, was a struggle. It wasn't just the online complications. The bigger issue was that I was a dyed-in-the-wool introvert who constantly struggled with crappy self-esteem. I didn't have the confidence or desire to go to bars alone. Even if I hadn't been working like crazy and spending all my free time with my daughter, finding a decent man in a dinky Canadian town was a little bit like plunking down two bucks for a lottery ticket seriously thinking you had a chance to hit the jackpot.

Still, you can't win unless you buy the ticket. With more optimism than I had a right to, I set up an account on the dating app Tinder. Dennis was one of the first guys to reach out and one of the few who didn't seem certifiably psycho or lust crazed. In fact, he was downright charming. We traded texts until we got to that point where you have to piss or get off the pot. We agreed to grab a drink at a pizzeria down the street from my apartment. I didn't really feel like going out, but I had been alone for almost a year. Sometimes you have to kick your own butt into action.

The Curious Café was a trendy new joint near where I lived. Cement floors, dark wood tables, gourmet pizzas, and a bar stocked with row upon row of craft beers. The place was mostly empty when I got there, so I took a stool at the bar and ordered a beer. Dennis walked in about fifteen minutes later. I was happy to see that his Tinder profile wasn't fiction. He was six feet tall, clean-shaven, with a full head of jet-black hair. He was lanky, stylish, and handsome. Great smile, no awkwardness.

He took the stool next to mine and ordered a pint. We picked up the conversation we had been having online. He told me about his business, a small financial services company that he made sound hugely successful. A big red flag popped up when he casually touched my leg and left his hand there. I thought it was an overly intimate gesture for someone who had only met me in person a few minutes before. But it had been a long time. He seemed like the whole package. I ignored my tingling spider sense, put the hand out of my mind, and got on with the night.

I'd been out of the game for what seemed like a long time. It felt so good to just get a buzz on and connect with a man who wasn't making crude suggestions by way of a messaging app. After the third beer, I realized I might be getting a little drunk. We decided to decamp for a local dive bar-slash-pub. They had a cover band playing rock hits from the nineties.

We danced and danced. Look at me, out on a normal date. I'm not a big drinker and was getting loopier as the night went on. It was a good, happy drunk, though, and Dennis seemed trustworthy. He was easy to talk to and I was physically attracted to him. I rarely take my clothes off on the first or even second date. Generally, it's a big event for me. That night was different. Maybe it was the long drought, or maybe he just seemed like the right answer to a question I had asked myself for so long: "Where the hell are all the decent guys in Kelowna?"

I invited him back to my place and we were barely in the door when we started peeling off each other's clothes and tumbling onto my unmade bed. We were physically compatible. All the lights were green and if the heavens didn't split wide open and angels start singing, it was still lovely sex. I'd be lying to say it was memorable; I wasn't the only one who was drunk. Regardless, it felt like chemistry. I woke up happy next to someone who seemed like a good thing. Had I found that mythical creature, the right guy? I so badly wanted to think I had.

We had breakfast and spent the morning cuddling on my couch. That kicked off a familiar pattern that I had established long before and would find incredibly hard to break. It's what I came to call my "anxious attachment." Once I decided there was a relationship to be had, someone who might accept me, I wanted everything to move forward at light speed so I could keep feeling wanted and secure. From that first date on, Dennis and I were nearly inseparable. He was happy to spend almost all our free hours together. For me it was security; for him it was a way to control me.

I had my pattern and Dennis had his. I didn't realize that I wasn't falling for the man, I was falling into the jaws of an illusion. I wasn't the only one of us with a confused identity.

Dennis was, I think, a type of con man. His one big talent was the ability to sell a fabulous cover story. Sadly, he conned himself as much as anyone else. He had crafted a spider-web fiction to lure people in, but he was caught in that web, too. He talked like some kind of super-successful financial investor, except that he was anything but. He was a player who rolled big in a BMW 7 series, shiny and newly waxed. Except it was just about all he really owned and he couldn't even afford to keep it tuned up. He had the clothes, the haircut, and the arrogance of someone who had lots and lots of money, except his bank account was on life support. He might as well have been someone's social media creation.

At least I knew I wasn't Instagram Jessica; Dennis had no idea that his whole personality was a mirage. That was a hell of a thing for him, and trouble for anyone who got wrapped up with him.

About the only sincere, authentic thing in his life was his adorable dog, a chunky, blue, Staffordshire bull terrier named Missy. In the end, Missy would create the few pleasant memories I'd take away from my time with Dennis. She woke me up each morning by jumping into bed for a cuddle, all four of her legs pointing straight up. No matter how bad things got, she always put a smile on my face.

Although I would eventually figure out the reality, early in our relationship I fed on the illusion. It was a little like how followers fed on Jessica, investing in the fantasy of her as a receptacle and outlet for their desires and dreams. Dennis meant security to me. Date after date, I told myself he could be the one. The trailer-park chick, the lost girl who wound up at a women's shelter, had won the lottery. I had finally found a safe place to put my heart. When we weren't together, I missed him. Hey, how about that? I was in love. It didn't matter if it was real, or true. It was close enough for me. Take that, Instagram Jessica. Three months later, lazing in bed on a Saturday morning, he said, "We should move in together. Get a house with a yard."

It was shades of Tyler, but I didn't let that register. Dennis was saying something I would have said eventually anyway. I imagined how nice it would be to wake up every morning next to someone who wanted me. Who had my back. Wasn't that family? I pressed into him. "Damn right, we should." I waited a beat just to enjoy the moment. Then pointed out the elephant I knew was lurking in the corner of the room. "But you know what I do for a living. I work at home and I'm going to keep my business going. It's always there." The one thing I would never give up for any man, was my income and my financial independence. I often thought about something I had heard when I was at the shelter: "Give a man the power to feed you and you give him the power to starve you, too." Being dependent on a partner for money would forever be a deal-breaker for me.

Dennis hugged me tight. "I don't care about that." He kissed the top of my head. "You know I think it's great. You made it on your own, I respect that." Wow. Could this really be happening? Had I finally gotten things right?

We started checking real estate ads the next day. By Monday, I was on the phone to a realtor. A week later, Dennis and I met up to look at different places. We came across a roomy if timeworn, four-bedroom ranch house in a sleepy, family suburb far from downtown. It had space enough for all of us, with a room I could use for what little camming I still did.

Truth be told, the house was suffering from a bad case of

neglect. The blue paint was peeling off the clapboard siding and a badly cracked walkway gave the property a dumpy feel that was the opposite of the vibe to which I'm normally drawn. It was a far cry from my bougie condo downtown. Generally, I roll more modern than traditional, but as we walked around the house I saw how jazzed Dennis was. I thought, "This is what it's all supposed to be about, right? Compromise? Building a future together?" I tried to see what he saw and teased out a few positives. A lot of room to spread out. A big overgrown front yard, and a patio and garden out back. It badly needed some tending, but there was potential. I could make it work. For him.

Here's the thing though: Date a Dennis, buy the illusion, and sooner or later the mask falls off. That doesn't happen by degrees. Just as guys are often shocked to learn that I'm not Instagram Jessica, I would soon discover that Dennis was not the stable, loving partner I was hoping for, much less the rock star he made himself out to be. Someone like him inevitably hits you with a sledgehammer wake-up call, a gut-punch epiphany moment when you realize you have slid down a greasy, slippery slope that once looked a lot like the Yellow Brick Road. Unfortunately, that moment is usually right after you've lost your footing. For me, that particular eye-opener was moving day.

The entire thing seemed staged by a hidden camera crew to reveal just how hellish the reality behind this man would be. It was like everyone except Jessica woke up that morning agreeing, "Let's pull back the curtain and drop the hammer!"

A gaggle of his friends showed up to help, but helpful wasn't the word that came to mind with this crew. Fortunately, I had hired reputable movers. They worked hard and, in no time, my place was emptied and the trucks loaded. At the new house, they got right down to business. Dennis's buddies managed to make the movers thoroughly miserable by either being in the way or, worse, "helping." They had swarmed the case of Molson's I bought, making short work of it and moving on to their own stash of booze. I said a silent thank you to the gods when the moving van was finally empty.

Dennis's chums took that to mean that the party had just started. Even drunk, they managed to hook up the stereo and blasted Fleetwood Mac. They destroyed the pizzas I ordered before the delivery guy was even out of the driveway. More beer magically appeared. Izzy retreated to her room. I did the same, closing my bedroom door, undressing, and laying down on the hastily made bed. The dogs opted to hide out with me and hunkered down at the foot of the bed.

I did the best I could to tune out the drunken yammering and hundred-decibel version of *Rhiannon* punctuated by even louder bursts of laughter coming from the living room. I had finally managed to suffocate myself with pillows into something resembling sleep when Dennis woke me up stumbling his pants off, stepping on Doc's tail, and literally falling into bed. Judging by the noise, the party showed no signs of winding down.

"Are they still here? I mean, at some point their going to pack it in and go home, right?"

"They're my friends. This is my house. You got no fucking

right to ask that." He was in his cups and I could see trying to reason with him was a lost cause.

"I just thought they'd call it a night by now. I mean, they're drunk and Izzy is trying to sleep."

"It's not all about you. You want to sleep, then go the fuck to sleep."

Okay then. Wake-up call delivered. I grabbed my pillow and blanket. Dennis was already snoring loudly by the time I headed to Izzy's room and laid down on the floor next to her bed. I tried to put the whole day out of my mind and get some rest. Moving days are always stressful, I told myself. You never see somebody's good side during a move.

Somewhere deep down inside, I wasn't buying my own argument. The fact that I had probably made another romantic mistake burrowed deep into my mind and stayed there. Staring at Izzy's night-black ceiling with the throbbing bass vibrating the floor underneath me, I knew that I had been treated to the real Dennis that day. I could no longer pretend to myself that the illusion of him held water.

Just the same, I also knew that I would cling. It was my pattern. I'd chew glass not to feel abandoned. Such a horrible thing to know about yourself, a prison I put myself in. I spent a restless night tossing and turning, with the worst thought you can have on the day you move in with somebody running on a loop in my head: "What the fuck have I done? Again?"

It's all too easy to stuff down those big life questions. The sun comes up, it's another day, things might change. Dennis' posse was gone in the morning leaving behind a hundred empty bottles and a completely trashed living room. But they were gone. Things could be normal now, I told myself. Izzy and I slowly unpacked boxes and tried to make the house our home. Dennis woke up at four in the afternoon, hungover and subdued if not sorry. That didn't matter; I was living with this guy and I was going to make the most of it. To start with, I had a business opportunity that I thought might be a fresh start, a wiping of the slate for Dennis and me to start fresh.

The most popular tattoo magazine in Europe, *Tattoo Life*, had reached out to me after seeing my *Inked* cover. They wanted me to be the cover girl of the year and do a calendar spread inside the magazine. Even better, they were going to fly me to London to be the face of the magazine at the London Tattoo Convention. Neither Dennis nor I had ever been to London, so we decided to make a European vacation out of the trip. We added stops in Amsterdam and Spain to the itinerary. I had high hopes that it would repair some of the damage the moving fiasco had caused, and that we would find our way to true north again.

I flew to New York for the *Tattoo Life* cover shoot and was stunned by how beautiful the shots came out. I struggled again with Imposter Syndrome, completely feeling like a fake as the talented photographer directed me to sit there, look out that window, stand like this. I was happy when it was done. The image the magazine picked for the cover was one of my favorites, and I couldn't wait to stand in the booth and scrawl my signature on it for body-art junkies and future Jessica Wilde fans.

The convention was amazing and impressive. It filled Tobacco Dock, a swanky convention center in East London. There was a pirate ship moored in the Ornamental Canal, a tiny waterway alongside the main building. The convention center itself was an updated industrial space that once served as an inland warehouse for a busy shipping port on the Thames. The building had two levels and caves underneath, and a crazy cool vibe. As if the venue hadn't been enough to spin my head, I turned a corner on my way to where *Tattoo Life* was setting up, only to find that they had hung a twenty-foot-tall poster of my magazine cover over the booth. Jessica was in the house.

Time flew by as I stood in the booth, signing autograph after autograph for all these complimentary fans treating me like I was some kind of celebrity. It was the first time I had ever been starstruck with Jessica Wilde. It was a tantalizing glimpse into what she could become, how big she might make it if I made all the right moves.

The three days I spent in that booth energized and inspired me. My time in London made it seem more realistic to entertain big dreams of places far beyond Kelowna and Canada. New York photoshoots. TV sound stages in Los Angeles. Jessica Wilde clearly had legs and could take me places with a little luck and a lot of hard work. Coming down off that high, watching them lower the poster and pack it up, I looked forward to the pure fun of exploring other European capitals with Dennis.

We both had a fascination with the hedonism of Amsterdam, and I was intrigued to check out the lifestyle and culture of Spain. We flew to Amsterdam from London. The moving day debacle seemed far in our rearview mirror and it felt like maybe Dennis and I were getting back on the same page. We hadn't spent a lot of time together in London because I was so booked up, but now we were just a couple on a European vacation. No schedule, no demands, just full steam ahead to fun.

Amsterdam was exactly what I thought it would be. I spent an afternoon checking out the Rembrandts at the Rijksmuseum and wandering the galleries of the Van Gogh museum because you can't be in Amsterdam and not visit some of the city's incredible treasures.

Mostly, though, we were there to sample the counterculture bits of a uniquely fast-and-loose city. The second night, we had dinner at a fantastic seafood restaurant. I drank one too many Smirnoff-and-sodas, and was a little wobbly by the time we left. We walked around and decided to stop at one of Amsterdam's famous coffeehouses—the local term for "weed café." I don't smoke pot, but we were both drunk and thought it would be a good idea to get high, too. It was not.

By the time we left the café, I was in no shape to process any more of Amsterdam's weirdness. Dennis, though, still had some sightseeing in him. He wanted to check out the city's world-famous red-light district, the area where prostitutes openly ply their trade. Amsterdam is progressive and prostitution is legal, but the red-light district is a flat-out strange scene.

The neighborhood itself is old-world quaint and charming, with narrow cobblestone streets and centuries-old buildings that could have been plucked right out of a snow globe. Strutting against that backdrop, beautiful prostitutes in revealing lingerie lounge in picture windows, seductively marketing their wares to tourists walking by. It would have been a sight at any time, but high as I was, it was surreal.

Five minutes in, I had seen enough. My head was spinning and I was already on the front end of what promised to be a rough night and morning. I just wanted to pack it in, hydrate, and try to sleep. Even sober, I wouldn't have realized that Dennis had other goals in mind. He was shopping. He checked out the price lists posted in the windows, describing what the women charged for different services. I leaned against a wall to steady myself as Dennis smiled at me. "I'm going inside."

Say what? My mind was working on quarter speed and I could barely process what he was talking about. Before it even registered, he waltzed through the front door of one of the brothels. I sat down on a stoop and tried to collect myself, wondering why the hell he would go into one of these places. He came out about five minutes later.

"What were you doing in there?"

He laughed. "I got a blowjob."

"What?"

"Don't worry, she made me wear a condom."

It takes a lot to shock me, but that did it. I got unsteadily to my feet and headed back toward the main district to grab a taxi to our hotel. Dennis trailed along, still checking out the women on display. When we finally got back to our room, it was all I could do to brush my teeth, peel off my clothes, and fall into bed. I woke up with sunlight burning right through my eyelids. I had earned myself a doozy of a hangover. The night before slowly came back to me, like bad mental snapshots flipping one after the other. Dennis was sitting at the tiny desk in our room. It took me a second to realize that he was scrolling through his phone.

Except, as I painfully and slowly focused my eyes, I could see it wasn't his phone. He was scrolling through mine. He saw that I was awake and pointed at the phone.

"Who the fuck is Ray?"

"Are you going through my texts?"

"Who the fuck is Ray?"

Who was Ray? It took a long few seconds for me to figure out who he could be. Then I remembered I had met a tattoo artist named Ray at the convention. He told me he wanted to do my next tattoo. Nice enough guy, Ray.

"Just some guy I met at the convention. He was trying to drum up business."

"I bet he was."

I rolled over and covered my head with a pillow. It was that first part of a time-slowing hangover where you know you have an incredibly long road ahead of you before you get to feel anything close to normal. It was going to be a minute-by-minute day. I just wanted to go back to sleep for a week. I couldn't though. We had a flight to Barcelona in six hours. I had no choice but to get out of bed and get myself moving, juggling a jumbo headache and a shithead, pouting boyfriend who apparently didn't know the definition of irony. He could drop fifty bucks on a blowjob from a hooker, but I was the one who was cheating because some random guy decided to shoot me a text?

That mess would ruin Barcelona for me. It was a beautiful city, if a little touristy. Any other time, I would have really jumped into the laid-back way of life and incredible food scene as a fun way to get out of my Canadian bubble.

It was damn near impossible, though, to get past everything going through my mind. I didn't want to be sharing a hotel room with the guy I'd come to think of as Mr. Red Flag, a walking four-alarm dumpster fire that I should have seen coming a mile away. I mentally beat myself up. I'd seen how greasy he was on the night we moved in together. I was stuck in my pattern, though, and I hated it. I would hold onto someone who treated me like shit because being abandoned by that person felt even worse. Dennis and I barely said ten words to each other the entire time in Barcelona. I counted the minutes until we could get on the plane home.

The flight gave me a lot of time to think, to process the hurt and resentment about what had happened in Amsterdam. I was far from clueless. I could see that the answer to my situation, what any sane and reasonable person would say, was: "You need to leave this jerk like your feet had wheels."

If only it were that simple. Those of us who are really damaged, I mean deeply scarred from what life has thrown at us over time, we get trapped by those scars. People like me harbor memories of the scariest, darkest hurt. It is a type of pain you never, ever want to experience again. In fact, I would go through a lot of other pain just to avoid it. My personal black hole, the place I wanted to dodge at all costs, was abandonment. The idea of being abandoned was so unnerving and disturbing to me that I would simply rather stay put in an abusive relationship than deal with being rejected and cast off.

Ever had a nightmare that lasted eleven months? That was the sentence I served with Dennis, locked behind the bars of my own neuroses and anxieties. False identities unravel quickly the closer you get and the more time you spend around them. It turned out that Dennis was not only a little scummy when it came to honoring a romantic relationship, but his "owning my own company" line didn't mean he actually had a viable business. Not surprisingly, he had burned a lot of bridges. Former clients weren't about to hire him again, and they were passing the word to potential new clients. Kelowna wasn't New York City. Dennis had polluted the small pool of clients and partners he might have counted on to get actual projects up and running. Within a month after we got back from Europe, he had no work at all.

He took it as an excuse to park himself on my overstuffed couch all day smoking pot, drinking beer, and watching daytime TV. It soon dawned on me that this wasn't a temporary condition. My boyfriend was just plain old unemployed. Had I only known that "investment tycoon" could so easily translate to "bum." I was paying all the bills and resented it.

"Maybe you should get out there and look for a job."

"I have a job."

"I mean a paying job."

"I don't know how many times I'm going to have to explain this to you. I own my own company. How's it going to look if I'm out there working for someone else? Nobody's going to take me seriously as a businessman."

There were so many things wrong with that statement that I honestly didn't know where to start. I had no response to that kind of delusion. As the weeks added up and turned into months, I realized I had saddled myself with another dependent mouth to feed. What's a girl to do? If your modeling career hasn't yet taken off and you're earning just a trickle of revenue from Instagram, you can't afford to be discerning. I revived my webcam work to pay the bills. Predictably, Mr. Blowjob was incensed. How could I share such an intimate part of myself with other men?

That the jealousy and possessiveness was familiar didn't stop it from breeding guilt. Everything was made worse by the fact that Dennis had plenty of time to stew. His days were spent sleeping in, smoking epic amounts of pot, and sleeping some more. He'd sit in front of the TV with a bowl of ramen noodles and a beer, and only look up when I took a break. He never missed a chance to shame me. I'd be greeted with a muttered, "Fucking whore," as I made myself lunch. I had to put that abuse out of my head because I was supporting all of us. I had to go into a room for hours at a time and be sexy Jessica, with a smile on my face doing things I would not have chosen to do. I couldn't give away any sign that there was an abusive man fifteen feet away who was making it his mission to be a leech on my bank account and curse to my self-esteem. That would have killed the illusion of Jessica and, along with it, my cam fees. If we wanted to eat, if we were going to avoid eviction, the show had to go on.

It is nearly impossible to explain how women get caught in traps like this. Part of the problem was that I didn't really believe I deserved better. Grow up with poor self-esteem and it causes all kinds of havoc in your life, but especially in relationships. I didn't believe I was worth being treated right, so I accepted things as normal that would seem utterly bizarre in isolation.

Instagram Jessica would never have stood for it, but where was she? A bunch of pixels on some screen. Meanwhile, the flesh-and-blood me struggled to pay the bills and tried not to think about the jerk in the next room who had no problem calling me the worst things you can call a woman. He said all that from the comfort of my couch, eating my food, under the roof and four walls I paid for.

I sucked it up because, well, guilt. Truth be told, I could understand a man not wanting to share that side of his girlfriend with other men. I didn't want to be camming, but it wasn't like I could float all of us by going to the mall and grabbing a minimum wage job folding shirts at The Gap. I essentially had two children. Bills galore. And, to be honest, I had become accustomed to a certain standard of living.

The whole situation was only made worse by Instagram. I was caught in the classic trap that plagues Instagram models and social media influencers. You have to tightly curate your posts so that you don't put your followers off. That means creating the illusion of revealing everything, when you're actually editing out significant parts of your life. Even though she would get a lot of screen time on my YouTube channel, I never showed pictures of Izzy on my Instagram page. It would have undercut the allure that was so much a part of Jessica Wilde's popularity. I was creating a character and a story through a series of images, one that men could place themselves inside.

Partly, it was giving the audience what they wanted. At the same time, it was a matter of control. My followers see only what

I want to reveal. I am always in control. It was one of those things that I found so attractive about social media; so many times in my life I've felt completely out of control. Not in my career, though. On Instagram and YouTube, I owned my destiny and I did it by controlling my image on a screen.

The trade-off is that I have to curate things. Jessica has to hit all the right notes to keep up the illusion that is key to nurturing followers' fantasies and drawing in new followers. Keep the eyeballs coming back no matter what. One seductive photo after the next. That's how I monetize what I do.

The funny truth? The vast masses do the exact same thing for free. They post pictures of kittens that aren't theirs, and sunsets they didn't really enjoy. The throw up posed selfies in an attempt to remake themselves as more popular, happier versions of who they really are.

My Instagram fiction was just more polished. It had to be an alluring lie, a continuity of deception. There are lots of other Instagram models that followers can ogle. The competition is amazingly fierce.

That's why I avoided ever posting a picture of Dennis and me together. It was a matter of business, but he saw it as a sign that I was being unfaithful—even though I was inside the house almost round the clock. Commonsense didn't figure into it; we were two exits down the road from reasonable, and he kept chipping away. The gems spilled out every day: "If you didn't spend so much time getting ready every morning to be a slut on the Internet, you could get a real job and not have to do this anymore."

Constant verbal and mental abuse can do a number on

anyone. It's sneaky, cumulative damage. I would sleep for an hour at a time, and then wake up in a panic, lost in the ether at three in the morning. What the fuck was I doing? How was I going to get out of this situation? How had I trapped myself like this? Again? The bedroom ceiling held no answers no matter how long I stared at it, exhausted. My skin was dull, and my hair had become brittle. My stomach hurt and I felt like shit all the time.

It didn't matter. What mattered was maintaining the illusion. I'd slap on my makeup, sit in that room, and turn on my fake happy face with my fake cheerful voice. I'd chat with some guy who was lost in his own world and badly needed to talk out his problems. If I wanted his money, I had to listen, really listen. I had to convince him that he was the only man in the world to me. I had to sell the illusion. Inside, I just wanted to curl up and weep.

I found an escape in the gym. I had always paid for a membership and made halfhearted attempts to bump around the equipment that lined the front half of the place. I would put a half hour in on the step machine without really achieving a workout. In that trying time, however, I learned that the gym could be a refuge. I joined a group of women working out with a trainer. It was a perfect outlet for my frustration and a positive way to refine Jessica Wilde even more. I hated it. The only thing that kept me coming back class after class was that I hated it ten percent less than I loved the cleaned-out, exhausted feeling of going home after a particularly brutal kettlebell session.

Meanwhile, Dennis continued his epic downward spiral. Six months in, we stopped even pretending that we had a sex life. We didn't sleep in the same room. I'd catch him in the garage at one in the morning, watching hardcore porn and doing cocaine—after having floated him another thousand dollars. My life had become a bad episode of the *Dr. Phil* show.

There comes a time when a trapped animal realizes it has to do whatever is necessary to escape. It turns into a simple matter of survival. A wolf chews its own leg off to get out of a steel trap rather than die of cold and starvation. I finally realized I was going to have to cut and run. There was no way I was getting Dennis out of that house. Why would he leave? Free food, free cable, free rent. Even if I could have evicted him somehow, through some superhuman force, it wouldn't have mattered. I didn't want to be in that shitty house anymore. I had never liked it there. It had never been home. I was in tears every day and the house was the physical placeholder for everything that was wrong, more battlefield than dwelling.

I started checking online rental listings. Unfortunately, Kelowna was booming. I couldn't find a crack shack for less than three grand a month. Finally, I contacted a realtor. Given the hot market, it just made more sense to buy if I could swing it. After loaning Dennis almost thirty thousand dollars over our time together, and carrying the household bills for a year, my savings were in tatters. I calculated I might have just enough for a small down payment. The realtor agreed to work with me and hooked me up with a mortgage broker who assured me a little magic could get me into my own castle despite my feeble resources.

The realtor quickly found an apartment she thought I'd like, on one of Kelowna's main streets. It was a cute, New York City-inspired condo building, only a few years old and in my favorite part of town. I picked Izzy up from school and waited for the realtor in front of the building.

She was late. The minutes ticked by. I got increasingly and unreasonably nervous, convincing myself that Dennis was going to drive by at any moment and see us standing there. I seriously thought about hiding in the shrubs. I could see him putting it all together, realizing his meal ticket was headed out the door. I imagined him disrupting my life and ruining things even more than he already had. When the realtor showed up, it took her forever to get the lockbox open. I stood behind her, willing her to get us inside.

"Doesn't she know," I thought, "that we could get caught right now? For god sakes, c'mon."

Once inside, I took a deep breath. It was a lovely apartment with two bedrooms, granite countertops in the kitchen, and brand new everything. My mind raced with possibilities. I could see myself waking up late on a weekend morning in the sun-drenched master bedroom with its cathedral ceilings, and then enjoying my morning coffee at the butcher-block island. It was the first optimistic vision of the future I had mustered in over a year. I heard, "I'll take it," and realized it was my voice saying those words. I gave the realtor an offer and told her how much I had to cover both the down payment and closing costs. I left with my fingers crossed that she and the mortgage broker could somehow make it work. She called before I even got Izzy home. She told me the offer had been accepted and that she could find me the financing I needed.

The snag was that the apartment had tenants. They still had two months left on their lease. Now I had a secret to hold. I thought that I had to make sure Dennis didn't learn about the apartment or he would figure out a way to ruin it.

Two months seemed like a small price to pay for my emancipation. Day after day, I played it as cool as I could and focused on steering clear of Dennis while I kept working and earning. He decided out of the blue to start growing pot in the garage. I couldn't believe he was putting my daughter at risk like that. I worked with Bobby so that Izzy spent the majority of her time at his place until I moved. I didn't feel like there was much more I could do. I just needed to hold on for a few weeks more. It became my mantra, "Not that much longer. Just a little longer."

Predictably, as the weeks dwindled into days, with the tenants scheduled to move out, I began second-guessing myself. It's yet another part of the vicious cycle women in mentally and emotionally abusive relationships struggle through. Regardless of how bad it might be, it's always the devil you know. Jumping into the unknown takes on an unreasonable amount of fear. It's so incredibly easy to get frozen into place. The same thoughts kept rattling around in my mind. What if things got better? What if he freaks out when I tell him I'm moving out? What if he tries to sabotage my move? Again with the "What if, what if, what if?"

Zero hour came and went. I was paralyzed with uncertainty, with pure fear. Fear of what, though? It's a question I've asked myself so many times. Dennis occasionally tried to physically intimidate me, but he had never hit me. Not even close. Ironically, if he had, I could have written him off and left without a backward glance. Instead, a month after the tenants had moved out, I was still living in that damned house wondering what the hell I was doing. Finally, after a brutal screaming match about Dennis' increasingly expensive drug habit, the expanding grow-light operation in the garage, and other issues, I knew it was time. I had to force myself to go. If not for me, than for Izzy.

I had long lost sight of the fact that people can surprise you in good ways as much as bad. So it came as a shock that none other than my adopted mother—the woman who had always been, in my opinion, the example of what not to do in parenting—showed up to be my savior. I had been bending her ear on the phone for months, talking through what was going on with Dennis, trying to make sense of it verbally. She was a good listener.

My mother might have had ulterior motives for supporting me, or perhaps it was just that she felt there was an opportunity to cement the bond between us, the connection that had for so long been frayed and tenuous. Whatever the reason, I needed help and she was there. When I called to tell her that I had to make the move that day, she was unconditionally supportive.

"I'll meet you at your apartment and we'll get you set up."

"You don't have to do that."

"Do you want me there?"

"Yes."

"Then I'll see you at the apartment. Don't worry, it's all going to be fine."

As Dennis stewed, I packed my car with a few essentials. I took my computer equipment and a quarter of my wardrobe and drove to the new place. I planned on picking up most of my other stuff when I could get to it without dealing with Dennis. I didn't yet have beds for Izzy and me. My mom suggested we go to Target and buy a couple of air mattresses. It wasn't the nest I envisioned, but it was a safe place. I could eventually buy new furniture if I needed to, but sanctuary is priceless. After all, I had slept on a cot just to have my place in a women's shelter.

Problem is, when you're emotionally fragile and someone's got their hooks deep into your psyche, it's not quite as simple as physically packing up your stuff and walking out the door. You're gone, but you don't just leave your abuser behind. Dennis wasn't done with me and I wasn't done with the fallout from the relationship. Not by a long shot.

After Izzy went to bed each night, I'd lock myself in the bathroom and hunker down in the tub for an hour-long crying fest. I couldn't have even described what I was crying about. All the mistakes, all the pain, all the frustration at not being able to figure out how to be loved and supported. Was I that worthless? Would it always be like this? In the end, all I knew was that I needed to cry and feel bad. It didn't help that Dennis began texting me a string of apologies, begging me to come back.

Abusive relationships are another identity scramble. Just like the confusion an online avatar can sow with the perception of a woman's real life, a guy who is adept at emotional abuse can absolutely shred a woman's self-image—even a strong woman. If you aren't with him who are you with? Can you stand alone? Are all the awful things this dirt bag is saying about you actually true? Is there even a kernel of truth in all that, something you haven't admitted to yourself? The doubts are the glue that holds you to your abuser; the ongoing abuse makes it harder to break loose.

So even physically separated, we started a long slow dance, a new pattern of abuse. He would call and say incredibly supportive sentiments. We would have long conversations about how things had to change if we were ever to go forward. We would go out on a date, and he would wind up back at my place. It would be nice for a night. I would start thinking that I had overreacted, that all the drama at the house was normal couple stuff. After all, I had never been part of a normal couple. It takes two to tango and I had played my part too, right?

By the next morning, though, it would be the same old Dennis. He'd find me in the living room, checking my Instagram page. He'd savage me with a dose of grief about how I was selling my soul, my body, and my right to live. We'd end up screaming at each other. I'd tell him to leave, swearing to myself I was done. I just would not listen to me.

In the meantime, work opportunities kept popping up. My relationship with *Inked* grew and bore fruit. In a moment of pure moxie, I proposed they hire me to write a monthly sex-advice column. I was stunned that they agreed.

Writing my "Wilde About Sex" column didn't pay well, but it raised my profile even higher. I was officially Carrie Bradshaw with tats and fake boobs. Even if five years of the same questions over and over (like the classics, "How can I get my girlfriend to go for a three-way?" and "How do I get my girlfriend to do anal?") would leave me with a rather low opinion of all men, it was a good brand-building gig.

Every little bit helps and you exploit all the opportunities that come along. For social media influencers, network relationships are symbiotic and essential. You promote a magazine and events, and the magazine and events drive followers to your social media pages. Win-win. When the publisher called and asked if I wanted to stand in *Inked*'s booth at the industry's biggest convention, the Golden State Tattoo Expo, I couldn't say "yes" fast enough. It would be a treasure chest full of Instagram, Facebook, and Twitter posts. It would be crowded with potential followers and potential business opportunities.

The Expo is held every year in Pasadena, California, and is sponsored by *Inked*. I love Southern California and the trip was a much-needed break from everything that was going on in Kelowna. Unlike the abuse I was still periodically enduring from Dennis, I was sure to enjoy positive feedback and support from fans and industry insiders. I thought it would be a clear and free getaway. Wishful thinking.

From the moment I touched down at LAX and turned my phone on, Dennis was blowing it up. Who was I with? Where was I staying? Wild accusations about me sleeping with random guys at the convention. Brutal text after text.

A woman's abuser doesn't need to be in the same room to do an immense amount of damage. I was in tears by the time the taxi pulled up in front of the Hilton Embassy Suites. Common sense tells you to shut the damn phone off. That didn't matter; I was still prey, locked under his control as I had been with Jason the pimp when I was twelve years old. So much time had gone by. I had grown up and created Jessica Wilde, but so little had really changed. I felt empty, powerless, and weak. I kept telling myself what I would have told any woman, "Block his number." The awful reality was that I simply, inexplicably, couldn't.

Parked in the booth at the Expo, signing photos for fans and being little Miss Smiley, was one of the hardest things I had ever done. I would have much preferred to find a good fetal position and wring out a body-shaking cry for an hour or two.

Luckily, I had bonded with a couple of other *Inked* cover models who could not have been better emotional rocks for me. Other women understand abusive relationships in ways male friends can't. You don't need to give them all the details; they can figure it out from a mile off. They know how hard it is to do something so simple as turning off your phone. There is a dark, irrational fear behind that, one that paralyzes you. Those models also understood the imperative of a good front, of making sure fans got their twenty bucks worth of face time with that fantasy crush they had gaped at in *Inked*. You don't drop that ball often and stay successful in my business.

A stunning model named Heidi Lavon buoyed me up with her cheerfulness and friendship. She was a pillar of support at just the right moment. Heidi and her boyfriend insisted that I join them for dinner with a group of industry pros. It was the exact opposite of what I felt like doing, and exactly what I needed. Everyone was so lighthearted and friendly, and Heidi made me laugh and laugh, until the tears were about something other than Dennis' abuse.

She and her boyfriend gave me perspective. By the time I sat down in my seat on the plane home, I knew I had to break loose of Dennis or go crazy with his crap. He had cast a jet-black shadow over what should have been a fun few days of work-cation. He was messing with my ability to build my business and was undermining what little self-confidence I had left. You set up a professional photo shoot to bank images for Instagram and you better show up knowing, in your heart of hearts, "Damn right I'm hot shit." Dennis was making that incredibly difficult. I knew all those things, and could even voice them to my mom.

For any abuse victim, though, there is always this mammoth gap between what you know and what you manage to do with that knowledge.

It took my daughter acting the champion to finally snap me out of it. Dennis had torn a tendon in his foot and had surgery to repair it. It fell to me, for some mysterious reason, to care for him. Why did I? Guilt, maybe. Or simply, I don't know. I went to the house we had shared and made him meals, cleaned the place, and made sure he was comfortable. He'd praise me for helping him, but I was always waiting for Mr. Hyde to rear his ugly head. It never took long.

One night, after he had healed enough to be mobile, he came over to my condo so that I could make him dinner. He was in a foul mood from the moment he walked in. Before I realized what was happening, he was laying the insults on so thick that I was sobbing uncontrollably on my own couch.

At the sound of the fight, my eight-year-old daughter bolted out of her room and shouted, "Leave my mom alone! Get out of here, right now."

He dismissed her. "Your mom is fine, kiddo. We're just talking about adult stuff. Get back in your room."

It was a moment of clarity, seeing this tiny little girl stand up to a six-foot-tall man for me. I stood up and inserted myself between them.

I said, "No, she's right. You need to go, now. And don't ever come back." It would be the last time I would see him.

It was an indescribably powerful relief to finally close the door on that ugly chapter of my life. To watch that bastard walk out of my condo knowing, absolutely knowing with certainty, that I would never let him back in.

I deleted his contact info off my phone that night. I felt like I could really breathe for the first time in almost two years. I was ready to leave his memory behind and turn the page. It was time to move forward and find the next mountain for Jessica to conquer, and to continue the search for real, true love. Mountains would turn out to be the easier conquests.

# -7-

# I WANT MOE

Our mothers hold a unique power over us and it's rarely a healthy thing. Even the toughest, most callous person finds it incredibly difficult to just walk away from her mother. Those women know us more intimately than anybody in our lives, which means there are buttons only they can push. Even though we weren't related by blood, my mother continued to wield that power.

Having come back into my life at a crucial moment and given me a lifeline of reassurance and support, it was difficult to hold what I perceived as old sins against her. I tried to get beyond the fact that she had chosen to live with someone I thought of as a pedophile rather than move out and surrender any potential stake in his assets. After all, she had ultimately lost out when the divorce was finalized and her lawyer failed to get her a piece of Martin's money or property. She had moved into a tiny apartment and her ability to find a new relationship, not to mention a man with money, seemed greatly diminished.

I suspected she had learned from the experience. People change, I told myself. Look at me. I had morphed from the aimless car wash cashier into driven Jessica Wilde. That creation was a completely different species than Tiffany. I put old wounds and grievances aside, let the past be the past, and let my guard down.

Here's what I've discovered. A person's basic nature rarely changes. Leopards don't swap out their spots for stripes, a turtle doesn't shed his shell and start sprinting through life, and one burst of compassion and supportiveness didn't mean my mom had suddenly evolved into Carol Brady or Mrs. Santa Claus. In fact, I strongly suspect that stepping up at that moment was a way to make herself a hero so she could bask in the light of adulation. I lost sight of the fact that with my mom, there was, in my opinion, always a bad bit of drama lurking around the next corner. We were having coffee one morning, Izzy playing in her bedroom, when she dropped a bomb on me.

"I talked to a lawyer last week."

"A lawyer? Why?"

"About my rights to Izzy. I want to formalize my visitation schedule. I want to have her every weekend."

Don't get me wrong, I've gone through some strange and bizarre moments in my life. That instant over steaming mugs of coffee, with the sun shining through my kitchen window? The moment when my mom told me that she was effectively going to be a third parent to Izzy? That made the top three.

"What? Are you nuts?"

Following our lifelong pattern, our voices got louder and louder. I was stunned as she almost shouted, "I have rights, grandparent's rights. I should get to see Izzy whenever I want. The lawyer thinks I have a case."

I snapped back, "Why the hell did you even go to a lawyer? Why didn't you just talk to me and Bobby if you want to see more of Izzy?"

"Because you're always cutting me off and excluding me from her life. I deserve my time with her. I'm a good grandmother and you've stopped me from seeing her before, for no good reason. You don't get to say when I can see her or have her stay with me."

"I cut you off and stop you from seeing her because you do batshit crazy stuff like this. You don't have the power or right to change the visitation schedule Bobby and I have. What's wrong with you?"

"You two can change your schedule easy enough. I do have rights. I do."

"You're nuts. You can get all the lawyers you want. You'll see Izzy when I say you can see her."

"You just want to punish me. You don't care if you hurt her, as long as you hurt me."

I stood up and pointed at my front door. "Get out."

I felt terrible rising to the bait, but I wasn't going to listen to anyone tell me they had control over my daughter. It would be a long time before I would talk to my mother again and I kicked myself for falling into our same old routine of punch, dodge, and counterpunch. The way I saw it, ultimately, it always had to be about my mother. It was her story; the rest of us were just characters in it.

My adopted mother had seemed to hold a grudge when I began to fully embrace the name Jessica. After all, renaming me right after she and her husband had adopted me sure looked like an exercise in ego. I don't think it ever bothered them that they had violated an agreement made with a vulnerable, emotionally distraught teenager. I wasn't surprised that she tried to claim some piece of ownership over Izzy. In my eyes, it was all about her, not Izzy. Understanding that didn't soften my disappointment that we were once again estranged. I vowed to myself to never put Izzy through what I had experienced with my mother. It wasn't pleasant, but it could at least be a lesson for me.

Putting the wall back up between us made me want to surround myself with genuine love. I had Izzy, who was pure joy. Maybe it was going to take some time to find Mr. Right and create my dream family, but in the meantime, I could bring a perfect dog into the mix. The one real purely positive aspect of my time with Dennis had been his pup, Missy. It was time for me and Izzy to have our own version of Missy.

I had moved on from my gym training group and hired my own personal trainer. I happened to mention to her how much I liked Staffordshire bull terriers, and complained that I couldn't find the breed anywhere in Canada. She turned me onto a breeder in Ohio. I contacted them as soon as I got home and, purely on gut instinct, I bought an eight-week-old puppy sight unseen. It would turn out to be easily among the top three best decisions I ever made. I picked the puppy up in Vancouver and named her Sophie. It seemed a fitting handle for a gentle, beautiful, fur-wrapped soul.

Sophie added a new warmth to the nest Izzy and I had

created. The puppy made my condo feel like a home, even in those lonely hours when Izzy was with her father and I had nothing more than comments scrolling on a screen to keep me company. There aren't a lot of tried-and-true cures for abandonment issues and poor self-esteem, but you can do much worse than latching onto a perfect little Sophie. She became and remains an outsized presence in my life, making me feel less alone. Walking her, talking to her, cuddling her, were all wonderful escapes from the work that lived where I did, and from the struggles with self-esteem and questions about who I really was that continued to haunt me.

Unlike camming—where you can make a lucrative income by putting in a couple grueling hours a day—earning a living on social media is a nonstop hustle that can take over your life. I don't care if you're a gamer streaming on Twitch, a home baker building a YouTube channel, or an Instagram tattoo goddess, you've got to feed the beast constantly. You're always working on content, or looking for other influencers you can connect with, or responding to followers. The workday grows longer of its own accord. Followers are insatiable. They want to click on your page on any given day, even any given hour, and find something new and sparkly. That's how the game works.

The other side to the equation is the need to constantly grow the overall number of those greedy eyeballs. The golden rule is to rack up followers, whatever it takes. If they ain't following you, they're following somebody else. You exploit any promotional opportunity that comes along. If you hesitate, it passes by. Even though I had built a decent audience for Jessica's Instagram page,

I knew it would be stupid to turn down any chance to pump up those numbers.

That made me a willing listener when the talent coordinator from the first adult industry camming awards show reached out to me. I was doing everything I could to leave cam work far in my rearview mirror. Camming had bought me a condo and put food on the table and then some, but it wasn't a pleasant way to make a living and I was focused on the transition away from it. After carefully considering the offer, I told the woman, "No."

I didn't see the point to diving further down the camming rabbit hole. Instagram and YouTube were the obvious future for me. I was racking up more and more followers every day by posting tasteful, alluring photos that didn't show so much as a nip. *Inked* looked like it could be a springboard, too. I loved working with the magazine and wanted to do more modeling. Long term, I saw myself maybe even breaking into the mainstream entertainment industry. I could see myself hosting a reality TV show. The XBIZ Cam Awards was not going to help me with any of that. So, when the award show coordinator called the second time, I turned her down again.

There didn't seem to be much point in doing a show that I wouldn't want to even mention on social media. After the third call, though, I got to thinking and ultimately gave in. There is a danger in turning down any promotional opportunity, and even a small chance that I would meet someone who was a mover and shaker in a more traditional corner of the entertainment industry. Plus, small towns close in on you every so often. I loved Kelowna but I was itching for a dose of a real city, somewhere they didn't roll up the sidewalks after dark.

The awards show was being held in Miami. I'd never been there, but I'd seen a lot of old episodes of *Miami Vice*. Palm trees. Pastel-colored Art Deco buildings flooded by cheesy uplights. White-sand beaches and turquoise water. In my mind, it was as far as I could get from the muddy shores of Okanagan Lake and frumpy downtown Kelowna.

Even better, the show was being held at the Versace mansion, which sounded like the height of cool. The talent coordinator put on a full-court press and sold the idea, promising I'd be treated like a queen. In the end, I didn't see the harm in being pampered and living big for a few days. After all, I rationalized, it wasn't a slide back into the actual camming; I just had to announce the award presenters.

As the plane banked into the landing approach for Miami International, I looked out of the business-class window and the Will Smith song, "Miami" popped into my head—*Everyday like a Mardi Gras, everybody party all day*. I took a deep breath. It felt like a big dose of freedom, a much-needed play break after those brutal final weeks spent slowly cutting Dennis loose and then grieving that I had. I was ready to unwind.

The show had booked me a sick room at a chic South Beach hotel where I ordered a twenty-dollar room-service cheeseburger, slipped into my favorite pair of ratty sweats, and tuned into the trashiest network reality show I could find for a relaxing night in before my big star turn.

The first thing on the schedule the next morning was to meet the main man, the guy who put the whole show together. I haven't come across a lot of people in my life who I would honestly say were stone-cold suave, but Moe defined the word. His name alone would have been odd on most people, but he pulled it off. Everything was working for him. He wasn't terribly tall, but he was one of those guys who is as confident and self-possessed as if he towered ten feet above everyone else. Darkly handsome, with easily the nicest haircut and most finely groomed beard I'd ever seen, he was style for real. The sexiest part, though? He was in total control. You could feel it. The type of guy who doesn't know the meaning of the word "flustered." Even though he looked nothing like the men I usually gravitated toward, it took all of about forty seconds for my crush to blossom. "Easy there, Jess," I thought, "Play it cool." At some point, there was going to be work to do.

Moe picked me up in a limo and the driver took us to the Versace Mansion. Along the way, we talked over how he saw the show unfolding. We settled into the mansion's lounge, an impressive space dripping with decadence. Overstuffed brocade furniture, arched floor-to-ceiling windows, and marble floors that amplified the thousand-watt Florida sunshine. I had to work hard at not letting my starry-eyed, Canadian, small-town bumpkin show through. Impressed? Hardly. Pure blown away was more like it.

I scanned through the notes the production coordinator had sent me, and tried to get a picture in my head of what that night would be like. What was I going to be doing minute to minute? I wasn't a professional presenter so the notes were little help; I could only figure out what award was being given when. There weren't even stage directions. I asked an assistant if I could get a teleprompter, and she said she would try.

Moe, meanwhile, sat with his laptop open and his phone pinging nonstop. His family owned XBIZ and he ran the whole shebang. He was cool as a cucumber giving orders, responding to texts, and settling down the production staff that kept rushing in and frantically peppering him with questions. It was just another day at the office for this Persian James Bond. I sat across from him, doodling notes and playing games on my phone. I snuck the occasional peek at the handsome stranger who seemed so completely above all the chaos around him. The man had game.

The afternoon faded into early evening and we made our way up to the green room. Ignorance is bliss. I had never hosted anything in my life and had no idea how unprepared I really was. If I'd been clued in that normally an awards show host does a full rehearsal and run-through, that it's normal to sketch out general comments and get a sense of timing, I might have been appropriately freaked out at my utter lack of readiness. Instead, I was calm when a wardrobe girl burst in to say that my dress had been stolen.

Without flinching, I said, "I guess we'll have to find another one then."

She relaxed, smiled, and quickly disappeared. Fifteen minutes later, she showed up with a sparkly black-and-gold number that fit me like a glove.

The hair and makeup pros arrived and set up shop. I was excited for Moe to see me all done up. I wanted to impress this guy. He had sat across from me—ignoring me—all day, while I lounged there with a clean, bare face, jean shorts, and a tank top. I figured I could turn his head with a glam makeover. I strutted out of the makeup room after the makeup artist and hair stylist had worked their magic, ready for the fawning to begin. Bring it on, good sir.

He looked me up and down and said, "Good."

"Good?" Are you kidding me? That was it? I checked myself in the mirror. Buddy, this girl is rocking. He had to be the coolest character I'd ever come across. I mean, "Good?" Please.

The crowd started filling the seats a little before seven. I mingled in the backstage lounge with other presenters, a dolled-up group of cam models. It was a fun collection of flamboyant personalities. I still wasn't focused on the work rumbling down the tracks at me.

As everyone else left to take their seats, though, it suddenly hit me like a truck. I was going to be leading this whole circus and I was anything but ready. No script, and no idea of what I was doing. Holy sweet mother of mercy! All I really had was a handful of barely readable crib notes and the moxie I was born with. Cue the panic attack.

I was overwhelmed by the Imposter Syndrome once again. Who thought I was capable of hosting an awards show? How had I gotten over on somebody that badly? My mind raced, and I was close to hyperventilating. I thought, "How the hell am I going to pull this off? I don't know my lines, I don't know any people out there, and this whole thing is just crazy." I felt so alone. Profoundly, desperately alone. Then, right when I needed him, Moe walked in to check on me.

"I'm sorry, but I don't know how I'm going to do this."

One more curveball for this chill operator. He was completely unruffled. "Okay, first, you need to breathe. Just calm down, everything's going to be fine. What would make you feel better right now?"

"A hug. And food."

He grabbed a large, plastic-wrapped brownie off the catered table in the lounge. He gave me an honest-to-goodness, "you have a friend in me" hug. Then he tore the plastic off the brownie and handed it to me. It was fudgy and sweet. As soon as I finished my first bite, I realized my teeth were now coated in sticky chocolate.

"Oh my god." I smiled at him. He laughed and gently wiped my teeth with a napkin.

"It's time to go. You ready?"

I nodded. I was the absolute furthest thing from ready but he gave me confidence and, hey, the show must go on, right? He led me to the staircase that fed down onto the stage. What seemed like the voice of God, boomed, "And now your host for the evening, the gorgeous Jessica Wilde!" I couldn't feel my legs as I somehow floated down the staircase onto the stage. I willed myself not to fall. I was sending Jessica Wilde out there to use her voice, but I had no confidence in her.

For the first time since I had created her, Jessica Wilde let me down. She bombed.

It quickly became clear that I was going to be scrambling to fill a lot of dead air. I can have a wicked sense of humor, but it takes more than a couple one-liners off the cuff to fill a series of three-minute gaps between a dozen presenters. I started poking fun at myself. Every joke, every jibe, fell short. It was a brutal crowd. You would think that people who were accustomed to stripping down and showing their most intimate bits on camera to complete strangers, would be easygoing. Perhaps even a little forgiving maybe.

You'd be dead wrong. I never felt so judged in all my life. I was waiting for the first overripe tomato to hit my dress. I wouldn't have been surprised if a cartoon hook had shot out from stage left to pull me into the wings. Frankly, I would have welcomed it. I learned that night what it means to die on stage. It's an ugly death.

That night was longer than any night has a right to be. Through it all, Moe was supportive, calm, and collected. He checked in with me between award presentations, talked me off the ledge, and reassured me that I wasn't doing as bad as we both knew I was doing. I was mortified, and he was nothing but kind, encouraging, and helpful. Who was this guy and where did I get one?

After what seemed like four lifetimes, the show finally and mercifully wrapped up. Moe appeared at my elbow, took my arm, and asked one of the backstage event photographers to take our photo. I threw on my Instagram auto-smile and thanked the gods that my boondoggle was in the can. He whisked me out to a car and the driver dropped me at my hotel.

Once I was safely in my room, I debated whether to even go to the afterparty. I mean, my sweats were right there, begging to be put on and covered in the crumbs of room-service food. Unfortunately, Jessica had obligations.

You learn through these experiences that a pro soldiers on. It would have been bad form not to show up at the party, even if I had to endure a holier-than-thou glare from some chick who had just won Best Fetish Clip. Besides, my work was finished. There was nothing left to do but screw the haters, put on a good face, and enjoy the rest of my night. That, and see Moe again. My crush had grown over the course of the evening and now had its own zip code.

The afterparty was at the glitzy South Beach venue, E11even Nightclub. The place was packed when I walked in but Moe materialized right in front of me as if I had thought him up. He was ever the gentleman, parking me in a VIP booth and getting me a drink. He sat by my side as we joked about the night's disaster, chain-drinking vodka-sodas. The combination of booze, the bizarre evening, and being surrounded by cam stars made me gutsier than usual. I am rarely the aggressor in romantic situations, but I decided to just lean in and kiss him. Thank goodness, he kissed me back like he'd been waiting for me to make my move all night.

Out of the ashes of my awards show performance rose the Phoenix of a romance. We danced all night. Eventually, we ditched the glitzy nightclub for a seedier, cooler setting. Moe told me he knew about a nameless underground club on the other side of town, the type of place only insiders can find. Having discovered a shared obsession with all things Rihanna, we sang boozy renditions of her greatest hits in the Uber on the way to the club. Although he was as patient as could be, the driver was perhaps less of a Rihanna fan by the end of the ride.

The guy dropped us at a dingy burger shack in what looked to be a bad part of town. I wasn't sure we were in the right place, but Moe seemed to know exactly where he was going. I followed him into the shop and we headed toward a throbbing hip-hop beat coming from the kitchen. There was nobody in the place and we strolled into a walk-in refrigerator and out through a door in the back that opened into a dark hall. With a whispered word to an ominously large doorman, Moe got us into the club. We picked up dancing where we had left off at E11even. Two hours later, we caught a cab back to my hotel.

Much as I thought he rocked, sex was not on the table. I was trying hard not to repeat the mistakes that had led me down the road with Dennis. Instead, drunk and exhausted, we burrowed into the amazingly comfortable hotel bed and simply cuddled away what was left of the wee hours. I kicked him out at ten the next morning so that I could shower and try to recover from a mega hangover.

He called that afternoon to invite me out to dinner with a group of other industry professionals, but Jessica Wilde was tapped. Girl had got her dance on and done her schmoozing. Besides, the industry pros at that table were working in a business I wanted nothing to do with anymore. It was time to recharge the introvert behind the tatted-up Instagram facade. I made an excuse that I hoped wouldn't hurt his feelings and opted for room-service chicken nuggets and chain-watching episodes of *Friends* on my phone.

I flew out the next morning. Long before the plane landed, I was missing Moe. That smile, and the peaceful serenity he gave off at all times. It was such a contrast to Dennis, and to all the men I had known. We started talking on the phone daily. He lived in Los Angeles and I made plans for a trip to California a month later. I tried not to let my heart run ahead of me.

I was incredibly excited to see him. I made my way through border security and was shocked to get pulled aside, into secondary control. A sweaty, fat boy-man ordered me into a back room and began to fire questions at me like I was an operative for Al-Qaeda Canada. He was the type of jerk with just enough power to get even with all those girls in high school who told him, "Not in a million years, pal." The type of guy who lives in his mom's basement and brags about his World of Warcraft scores.

The first thing he asked me before bringing me to the dingy windowless room was who I was visiting and why. I made the mistake of telling him Moe's full Persian name and that he had hired me for an awards show. It was the worst possible choice of words. I hadn't got paid, but my expenses were covered and it was great exposure, so I thought of it as a gig. Border officials, though, have red flags about foreigners coming into the country to work. I didn't have a work visa. Some chick with sleeve tattoos and a hot body coming to "work" in the states was bound to raise alarm bells that lead to interrogation rooms with overweight police academy rejects questioning you for hours.

"Are you a prostitute?"

"What?"

"Are you a prostitute? Is he your pimp? Are you coming into the United States for sex work?"

"Are you nuts? I'm going to visit a guy I like."

"Are you carrying drugs in your luggage or anywhere on your person or inside."

"You're kidding, right? You think I'm a drug mule?"

"Just answer the question."

On and on it went. Never argue with a badge. You'll only give them a reason to slam the door on you. Finally, after I was driven to tears of frustration, anger, and exhaustion, the inevitable decision came down. "We find reasonable cause to deny you entry to the United States today."

Moe seemed further away than I could imagine. I called him as soon as I got home. He was as reassuring as ever. "Another day. You'll get through. We'll be together."

I had finally found this gem of a man, this giant among midgets, and an over-amped border security system is going to stop us from seeing each other?

Oh, hell no.

I spent the next six months dealing with lawyers and border security officials, trying to fight my way back into the United States. I had been put on the no-fly list, stuck in a maze of red tape and bureaucracy. Moe and I started Facetiming every night. Yet another part of my life lived through a screen; we were falling in love by way of digital projections. It was less than satisfying.

Finally, I tried to get into Los Angeles again. My lawyer saddled me with an enormous blue binder full of bank statements, tax documents, and pretty much every single paper tied to my life in Canada. There was even a copy of the deed to my condo. I headed to the airport and was completely shocked when, after an hour of the same questions and trotting out my binder, they let me through.

I called Moe from the sidewalk in front of LAX arrivals

terminal, yelling into the phone. "I'm here. I got through."

"Finally! I'll see you in a few minutes."

It was like a dream come true. He continued to be a perfect gentleman. His apartment was just as I imagined it would be: elegant, comfortable, and tasteful. There was a small part of me—gun-shy Jessica—just waiting for the other shoe to drop. After two days, I expected to wake up next to him and hear, "You're a slut. You need to do everything differently." But that wasn't Moe. For the first time, there was no other shoe.

Far from being ticked off when I had to post on Instagram or respond to comments on YouTube, he was supportive. He encouraged me to shoot for the moon. Moe had years of business experience under his belt. He was like a caring lover, understanding friend, and insightful adviser all rolled up into one. He guided me in decisions about social media promotion deals, new business opportunities, and building my personal brand. He even built my website. It was the first time a man had ever encouraged me in that way. It felt like as long as I had him in my corner, the sky was the limit.

My fascination with tattoos had long led me to wonder if some niche of that industry could possibly be a Plan B for me. Moe encouraged me to explore that because we both knew that there was an expiration date on modeling. Nobody puts a fifty-year-old tattoo model on the cover of a magazine. I wanted to get out ahead of that transition.

Although I have no artistic ability, I do have a good eye for makeup and styles. There are types of semi-permanent tattooing called micropigmentation and microblading (for scalp and eyebrows respectively). The first is a solution for balding men who don't want to or can't get hair plugs. The latter is a way for women to have semi-permanent, perfectly shaped eyebrows.

I bounced the idea off of Moe and he thought it had a lot of potential as a business. I took the leap and rented a small storefront in Kelowna, opening the business as Inked Cosmetic. I figured I could try it out in my hometown. If it was a success, I would eventually move it to L.A. I quickly built a solid roster of clients simply by spreading the word on social media. I made a decent profit from the first month.

I loved getting out the house yet still having control over my work hours. I didn't take walk-ins, and didn't schedule appointments before noon or after five, to make sure I could get Izzy to school and pick her up. I balanced my new business schedule with regular visits to Los Angeles every chance I got. It was hectic, but it was worth it. I'd lug my gigantic binder along like a traveling buddy, making the trip with the certainty that I was falling for Moe.

Love was coming to mean something different for me. I needed a partner, someone who could roll with the way I made a living, and separate the real me from Instagram Jessica. He got it. He cared about the real me.

It wasn't a traditional relationship; more like a team of two who collaborated on romance, business, the whole shebang. I could so easily envision a life with him. It would be the three of us, Moe, Izzy, and me, creating a wonderful world of our own in Los Angeles. I could move Inked Cosmetics there. I would leave even the memories of camming behind as I grew Jessica beyond all that, to a bright and shining future.

Smarter people than me said it long ago: Man plans, God laughs.

I had taken a day off to go with my friend Jerry to the lake. We spent a couple hours of a lovely warm day staring at the water and hanging with some of his pals. On our way home, a teenager who had just gotten his license, ran a stop sign and T-boned Jerry's car. I only registered the other vehicle at the last second and it felt like a bomb had gone off right outside my door. Even with my seatbelt on, my body was jackknifed sideways as the passenger's side was caved in by the nose of the other car. At first, I thought I had been lucky and escaped uninjured. It was only the next day, when I could barely move, that I realized something was very, very wrong.

My shoulder was killing me. I took a long bath and tried to rest, but I couldn't get comfortable. I had two appointments at Inked Cosmetic that day and that's when I realized the injury was more severe than I had thought. I could barely hunch over to work on a client; my whole upper back and neck would screech in four-alarm pain. I found a good doctor who ran a battery of tests. The results showed that I had torn and damaged my right shoulder rotator cuff. Surgery was an option, but I wanted to avoid that. Instead, he connected me with a talented physical therapist. We made progress, but I was still in excruciating pain whenever I sat in the chair to work on clients. Eventually I had to throw in the towel and admit I just couldn't do the specific physical work Inked Cosmetics required. I reluctantly shut the business down.

It was the end of Inked Cosmetics, but just the beginning of my journey through the country of injury-stan. The neck problems that grew out of my shoulder issues became chronic. It would ultimately mean years of physical therapy. My therapist gave me a program of exercises that I incorporated into my gym routine. My neck, though, would never be the same. I developed an autoimmune response to the trauma, and began a long-term battle with chronic fatigue and joint aches.

All that made traveling to L.A. even more of a slog. I realized that Moe was as close as I had come, and would probably ever get, to the perfect man. They say that "absence makes the heart grow fonder," but I can testify that distance can kill a relationship. At first, it had been fun and exciting jetting off to L.A. every couple of weeks. There was always an intense longing and anticipation made worse by talking on video chats. He was right there, but he wasn't. Over time, the simple reality of geography and borders wore on our relationship, like water eroding a rock. The anticipation that was so exciting at first, now became a frustrating exercise in endless waiting and a constant reminder that what I wanted the most was being kept just out of reach. I had the added misery of neck and shoulder pain from plane seats that weren't exactly designed with ergonomics in mind.

What I didn't really understand through all of that was that a relationship like ours only worked if there was a clear end point, some shining goal at the other side that would keep both people moving forward.

We didn't have that. Moe was swamped running a highly successful, high-stress business and simply couldn't get away. I was racking up huge travel bills and was having a harder and harder time leaving Izzy and Sophie to rush through a whirlwind four-day weekend. I'd get home almost crippled by neck pain. It all took its toll. I had a business to run and a daughter to raise. I didn't know what to do. Was I just going to keep running off to L.A. every chance I got? Would that be the sum of our romance, a week here and three days there? I wanted to build a life with him, but he may as well have been on the moon.

The answer was obvious and excruciatingly painful. I would never have made the decision myself, because it was like accepting abandonment was my permanent condition.

Ultimately, it turned out that the best guy I ever found actually did have a flaw or two. The more we talked about what lay ahead, the more I pushed for Izzy and me to move to the States and live with him, the more it became clear that Moe had commitment issues. He wasn't willing to go all in on that obvious solution. In fact, I could tell the idea kind of panicked him. Much as we talked and talked, we couldn't talk around the reality that he wasn't sure he wanted an insta-family. The whole thing came to a crashing conclusion on a Facetime call.

He seemed off, not himself and preoccupied. Finally, he said what the look on his face was already telling me. The last thing in the world I wanted to hear. "I can't do this anymore. You have to find someone you can have a life with. It's not me."

"Why not? I love you. You said you love me."

"I do, Jess. I just can't do this. It's too difficult and it's not going to work."

We ended the call and I felt the floor fall away under my feet.

Even though I was smart enough to know that our romance could not survive just stumbling forward the way we had been, I had totally duped myself into thinking that somehow we would work it out. I had assumed that some unforeseeable great big event would happen to save everything. I mean, if both of us were in love, how could it not work? I was so frustratingly close to what I had desperately wanted for as long as I could remember.

The loss haunted me as I spiraled into an all-too-familiar grief. More tears, more pain. The couples I saw happily walking hand-in-hand through downtown Kelowna, leaning into one another and sharing laughter and smiles, they mocked me. Again. What secret did they know? It was like a magic trick I couldn't figure out. Why did it have to be so damn hard, love?

At first, I was devastated. I couldn't even talk to Moe. I wouldn't respond to his texts or emails. Each one was just a stabbing reminder of what we wouldn't have, of being abandoned yet again. That wasn't how it really was. Moe wasn't like Dennis or any other man. Our love remained, even if that just added to my confusion. Ultimately, we began talking again. Moe would remain my closest friend, but the experience reinforced that it was time for me to learn how to be strong on my own, to discover who I really was under the layers that I presented on social media.

I dove back into work, embracing the familiarity of posting. Now, though, I looked at everything through a new, more critical lens. I wasn't going to be sucked in anymore; I was going to be in the driver's seat of my career and my life. I was going to own Jessica Wilde, not the other way around.

# -8-

# INSTA-VALIDATION

Instagram Jessica steadily racked up followers, including more than a few celebrities. The younger me might have been starstruck by big-name actors showing me some sugar in an Instagram direct message. I wasn't that girl anymore. Now I understood how easily men latched onto a sultry fabricated image and projected their fantasies onto her, convincing themselves she was real. No Hollywood star was reaching out to *me*. They were grabbing at their version of Jessica Wilde and whatever self-serving fictional backstory they had manufactured about her. Short guys? Jessica has a hidden thing for short guys. Country boy? Ah, he knew, just knew, Jessica was itching to drop the glamour act, slip into some Daisy Dukes, tie her shirt in a belly-button knot, and get her cowgirl on. City mouse? Same song, different melody. Instagram Jessica was, and always would be, a blank canvas for fantasies.

Actors proved to be no different from other men. Funny enough, they were in the same boat I was. They were skilled at weaving illusions, at creating different versions of themselves for the press, for their fans, and for the roles they played. That didn't stop them from ironically falling prey to the myths they created. A couple of box office hits and a tide of adoring fans were a funhouse mirror. The characters these guys became most famous for turned into the men they saw in the mirror every morning. I could have told them, you make a handsome living off a lie, a cardboard alter ego, and sooner or later you're going to lose sight of the flesh-and-blood person behind that illusion. That fake image becomes a wall between you and the ability to connect with other people. Been there, was doing that.

They had it worse than I did. They weren't just stuck in an ugly social media feedback loop. Their illusions were bought and sold worldwide, splashed across billboards, thrown up on big screens, and popping up in toy stores and comic book shops. As much as I wrestled with Jessica Wilde, I could only imagine what it was like to stay anywhere close to grounded and hold onto a healthy perspective of self under the weight of all that. See your own likeness in an action figure? It had to create a perverse, surreal worldview and, in turn, a warped view of others.

None of the celebs that DM'd me on Instagram were interested in an actual woman. They were too busy looking to validate their ever-growing egos and feed the myths and false identities they had adopted.

Who could blame them? I only had my internal dialog; their false identities were hungry monsters fed by millions of rabid fans, bootlicking representation, one-dimensional studio execs, and a merciless entertainment machine. These guys, they were all looking for ego strokes. They *were* the illusion. They desperately needed to prop it up and avoid facing the lonely, self-doubting lost boys underneath. They thought I'd play the game like everyone else, that I would fall all over myself fawning on them. That I would jump into bed with them at the drop of a two-thousand-mile digital booty call.

Like so much that men assumed about Jessica, they missed the mark by a country mile.

I traded texts with a couple of celebrities out of pure curiosity. One of them was an A-list action hero. Fictions of identity go both ways, and I'm as prone to buying into my own version of an illusion as anyone might be. When he first reached out, I formed a picture of this actor in my mind. I envisioned a pampered man-boy rumbling around in some overdecorated Brentwood mansion, living his star's life where nothing was ever wrong.

I only had the two-dimensional portrait painted by the characters he had brought to life on screen to work with. I wondered what he was really all about underneath that pretty façade, the one the studios built up in trailers and promotional interviews. Who was he, really? The truth would be a bit of a disappointment; some people's true self is actually the darker underbelly of the sparkling illusion they present to the world.

We agreed to chat on Facetime. He was brash and cocky out of the gate, like he was doing me a favor even agreeing to talk to me. In fact, he seemed to be compensating for something. Maybe because he was short. Maybe because he wasn't Tom Cruise. I doubt even he knew. If our chat was any indication, he was the furthest thing from self-aware. Finally, after ten minutes of chatting about all the great things that were going in his life, he got to the point.

The pitch: "Come to L.A. We won't be able to go out, but we can have a lot of fun right here."

He gestured to the vague background of the nondescript room behind him. The man did not have a decorating sense; it might as well have been an Embassy Suites. Brentwood mansion, my ass.

"Why wouldn't we be able to go out?"

"The paparazzi would swarm me. Trust me, we could walk into a bar together and you could be butt naked with a sign around your neck that says 'fuck me,' and no one would look at you because I'm an A-lister."

If I was going to trek to L.A., it would be to see Moe. Moe was real. He was dashing, caring, smart, funny, deep, and well-adjusted. Moe was human and flawed, substantial and a complete person. More than anything else, he was comfortable in his own skin. Moe knew who Moe was. This guy on my laptop screen? Please. It was all I could do to not burst out laughing.

I let him down gently because I knew better than anyone how easy it is to fall prey to your own illusion. I'm sure he moved onto the next target and the next, trying to fill a hole that couldn't be filled, because the hole is part of the illusion.

He was far, far from alone. Social media has always made self-delusion as easy as creating a screen name. Problem is, most of us don't look at it from the other side of the screen, so we don't realize how fake our online identities become. That divorced dad posting a cascade of smiley pics with his kid on a camping trip?

He wants to believe—needs to believe—as much as he wants all his friends to believe that he's an engaged super parent. Even as he plops his daughter down in front of the TV for the third night in a row, for yet another coffee-table Happy Meal dinner. The dozen "likes" he gets on that Facebook photo feels good and quiets the self-criticism and doubts. Those likes are, for everyone, a fix. You don't have to be a junkie to know that the fix you just had leaves you craving the next one.

That's the bitter truth. We think we want deep meaningful connections to other humans. We think we want to be the people we portray on social media, that those half-truths and fictions are going to make us happy.

Sadly, those are just unsatisfying echoes.

Professional influencers aren't immune. There are literally hundreds like me on Instagram. We all kind of look the same, Instagram models. Yet it really feels like unique validation all my own, that dubious dopamine surge from the fifty thousand likes a bomb-ass photo pulls in. Total strangers hyping me up, verifying … what actually?

There's nothing like that surge. Well, maybe heroin. I know it's not real, but I want it so bad. *They like me. They think I'm beautiful. They support me.* I can check a photo I've posted forty times in a day, just to read the comments, see who liked it, and bask in the Insta-validation.

Yes, that girl in the photo is not me. That's not how I really look because it's not a candid image. But, wow, it sure feels like honest-to-goodness love for the former car wash cashier girl who wanted nothing more than to be the beautiful princess. Then the withdrawal starts, because the buzz never lasts. The next day, that's just an old post, forgotten. The comments dwindle. I need to feed the habit. Onto the next post, chasing the dragon to re-create that rush. And the next, and the next.

An addict knows she's an addict. Junkies don't really think they are on top of the world. Almost from the time I set up my Instagram account I understood the perverting effect social media had on identity. I made good money manipulating that sugar-coated surreality.

Unfortunately, it was always going to make finding love an incredible challenge. I was still hopeful, even if my personal history mocked me. I mean, I had gone through the truly awful losers and that didn't work. I had gone through the prince of my dreams, and that had not stuck. I wasn't sure what to try next. I knew for sure that any man I went out with would now have to measure up to Moe. A successful confident man who treated the woman on his arm as an equal. It was an awfully high bar.

The problem was that any potential candidate would inevitably head right to Instagram or YouTube and decide I was Instagram Jessica. The same reaction that bred all those comments that were my version of opiates, were responsible for love-blocking me from making a deeper connection with a potential significant other. Guys would see Instagram Jessica and weave a tidy little fantasy in their heads. They'd envision that enchantress catering to their every whim and tolerating all their flaws. That was what any guy reaching out expected me to be.

Even though I knew all that, I didn't know how to get around it. The heart doesn't stop wanting what it wants. I was lonely.

That loneliness was only made worse when I scanned my social media pages and saw all the guys commenting and engaging with the illusion of Jessica Wilde. How they loved her. Me? I had a bazillion followers and three friends in real life. It struck me as bitter irony that the one relationship I had come across that ticked all the boxes a girl could want checked off had been eighty-sixed by fate and geography.

I mean, c'mon. Where was the justice in that?

As I was pondering the social media life, real life intruded. The woman who had told me who my birth father was, sent me a text. "I'm sorry to give you this news, but I thought you'd want to know. Your dad died." She included a link to the obituary. He had OD'd on cocaine.

I was strangely distraught at the news. I had opted not to connect with him when I had the chance. Now I'd never have that chance. He would never know his daughter and granddaughter. I would never know what he might have told me about my birth mother. The sense of loss stayed with me. I couldn't let it go. I decided to contact his parents and learn more about the family I could have had.

I was nothing if not great at stalking people online. I dove into researching his connections and eventually tracked down his mother, a woman named Bev. I called her. Without thinking through all the potential consequences, I told her that I was her son's biological daughter. He had never told her about me. She was thrilled at the news that she had a granddaughter. Why wouldn't she be? A piece of her son lived on.

Bev was a lovely woman. She didn't hesitate to respond and engage. She wanted to connect and establish a relationship. We spent hours on the phone as she described a family I couldn't have imagined. I had uncles, cousins, nieces, and nephews. It was like finding buried treasure in your backyard. The more she described the family, the more excited I became. Family. I had searched so long, and here it was, waiting for me the whole time.

Bev and I agreed that it was prudent for me to take a DNA test before I jumped into getting to know her family. We wanted hard evidence for any naysayers. It made total sense to me, because I was certain that the result would be exactly what I wanted it to be.

I ordered a DNA test kit. A few days later, a small white box arrived in the mail. It contained a large plastic tube with a bar code sticker and tight-fitting lid. There was a booklet of instructions, but the process was as easy as it was gross. I had to spit in the tube over the course of an hour. Then I boxed up the sample and sent it back. Bev, meanwhile, sent in her own sample.

Bev and I continued to talk and get each other even more excited. Bev planned on making the trip to Kelowna with other family members to meet her long-lost granddaughter in person.

The DNA tests, meanwhile, seemed to take forever. Weeks went by and I became increasingly impatient. Finally, one morning I opened my mailbox to see an envelope with the testing company's logo on it. My heart felt like it would beat a hole in my chest. I rushed inside, tossed the rest of the mail on the kitchen counter and looked at the envelope. I had Bev on speed dial, ready to pass along the good news. I tore open the envelope, unfolded the single sheet of paper inside, and read the short, heartbreaking sentence. There was no DNA match. I had found my father. I had lost my father. I had mourned him. Now I had lost him in yet another way.

I called Bev and told her what I had just read. She took it as badly as I did. She sounded heartbroken, but there was now no reason to meet. I had lost a family, along with the notion of my father. A fake out. Another illusion. What was worse, I was now back to square one. I had reached out to everyone who might have known my mom and the only lead I got was dead wrong. There was nowhere else to turn. I resigned myself to the fact that my biological father would forever remain a mystery to me.

I hadn't really lost anyone in that whole transaction, but it sure hurt like I had. It felt like a piece of me had melted away, had just disappeared. Having never known my biological father it seems silly to say, but I felt abandoned yet again. My real father had disappeared into the mists of time. It wasn't the only cruelty that "time" was inflicting. My thirtieth birthday was rearing its ugly head.

Age is the enemy of any model, but especially social media models and influencers. I knew me. Turning thirty could have easily been a dangerous, scary, dark rabbit hole for me, a place where loneliness and bulimia joined forces to throw me off balance for weeks. I needed to keep busy and think as little as possible about my entrance into the over-thirty club.

I jumped at the chance to book a gig hosting a tattoo

convention in Victoria, British Columbia. It seemed like a good opportunity to distract myself. I had a casual friend named Heather, a talented tattoo artist who was attending the convention. I mentioned that it was my birthday and she told me she wanted to throw me a birthday party on the second night we were there. You don't turn down a networking opportunity, but I was far too jaded not to face the truth. A birthday party, a real celebration, happens with friends and family. A party in a hotel bar? Another illusion, full of industry people who knew little about me beyond the ink on my skin. Most of them didn't even register that it was my birthday.

I made the rounds, smiled my Instagram smile, and called it an early night. I opened the door to my hotel room and got punched in the nose with the smell of flowers. My Hilton suite had been turned into a garden kaleidoscope of flower bouquets. As I made my way through it all, I discovered a small feast of room service desserts on a cart—everything sugary offered on the hotel's menu laid out in an enticing display.

Moe. He never forgot, and never failed to surprise and impress me. I was struck for the millionth time with the curious mix of joy that he was my friend and my rock, and frustration that we had failed to make it more than that. Just like the chocolate torte he'd had sent to my room, it was bittersweet.

I slowly nibbled on a cookie and channel surfed through the available TV options. I couldn't focus and turned it off. I looked around at the multicolored roses, jewel-toned dahlias, and wispy baby's breath. I thought about where I was, and what the next decade of my life looked like. I had assumed that by the time I turned thirty, I'd be deep in a relationship with someone like Moe. I had envisioned a life full of love, laughter, close friends, fun, and family.

Instead, I was single and alone, surrounded by people who had no idea who I really was. I was working my butt off and getting older in an industry that revered youth above all else; I had never been more aware that my career had a shelf life. I had to have a plan B.

Those realizations followed me home. I sat at my living room desk lost in the thoughts that had begun in a flower-filled hotel room. Aging was the mortal enemy of my career. I felt a little shudder of fear, of losing everything to the march of time. Sliding back into the trailer-park poverty that I had fought so hard to shake off. I needed an idea.

Sophie snored from her usual spot on the couch. I sat at my desk looking at a copy of *Tattoo Life* with my photo on the cover. There was something about it, how even though it hadn't been my first shoot, it was still so thrilling to get that cover. It never grew old. Then it dawned on me; that wasn't my excitement alone. Every influencer and tattoo model I knew was ready to kill for a cover. Every single one of them. That smelled like a competition. There were so many gorgeous tattooed women clawing for the same career. Why not a reality television show pitting those chicks against one another for the prize of being on the cover of *Inked*?

As TV went, it could be super edgy, cool, and sexy. It seemed a natural in an entertainment landscape where the tattoo-based reality competition TV show *Ink Masters* was racking up season after season of high ratings and even spawning spinoffs. I knew I could totally pull it off. It could be my stepping-stone into TV and mainstream entertainment. A future beyond Instagram Jessica. That idea seemed so alluring, so reassuring. I shot *Inked*'s creative director an email. Thirty minutes later, we were on the phone. He loved the idea.

"Let me pitch it up the ladder and get back to you."

Then ... nothing. I waited and waited. Eventually, I figured it had simply died on the vine. Ideas were pitched all the time. Precious few made it to reality. Most were killed on the spot. Some, like mine, lingered and were ultimately just starved to death and ignored. I started mulling over other ideas. I hadn't had any epiphanies a month later, when I got a message from some random stranger who had found me on Instagram and wanted to know if I would be interested in entering a competition to be the next *Inked* cover girl.

Say what?

The magazine had run with my idea, turning it into an online promotion rather than a TV show. I called the marketing company that was putting the competition together for *Inked*. I told the manager handling the promotion that it was my idea and I hinted at legal action. He offered to make me the host of the competition, which was really the launchpad I was looking for in the first place. In business, there isn't room for bad feelings or revenge. People and companies do messed-up, underhanded stuff. You roll with the punches and run with a winner. I took the gig. Just as I knew it would, the competition proved to be a boon for my social media profile and my business cred.

If only I had done so well in my personal life. I had half-heartedly gone back to Tinder and ventured out on a few dates, but it was hard for any man to make a dent in my memories of Moe. I wound up most Saturday nights, working far too long, curling up on my couch with Sophie, watching *PS I Love You* for about the hundredth time, and slobbing out. I couldn't have been further from the sex queen on Jessica Wilde's Instagram feed. Those nights, I would do what I could to forget that she even existed.

One night six months after my thirtieth birthday, I was going down blind alleys on Instagram, checking out cute guys. I came across a mixed martial arts fighter who lived in Calgary. He was built like a welterweight brick house, with a square jaw, military haircut, and devilish smile. I promptly hit the "Follow" button and shut it down for the night.

There's a certain cat-and-mouse game to Instagram flirting. If I followed him, then he was supposed to follow me. I'd like a picture of his and he'd like a picture of mine. So on and so forth until one person finally texted the other. This guy was clearly new to the game. I woke up the next morning to find an Instagram message: "You better not unfollow me now."

Matt and I ended up connecting in an old-fashioned phone call. That started a string of nightly Facetime sessions. We hit it off. It was incredibly nice to have an adult I could talk to on a regular basis again. Well, technically an adult.

I was keenly aware he was only twenty-five. Five years difference might not seem like a lot, but it's all in the perspective. I'd been on my own since I was sixteen; Matt lived with his parents. He told me it was a transition, that he had broken up with his girlfriend a couple months before and they had sold the house they owned together. He had moved home to get himself back on track, continue training, and find a new place to live. As red flags go, it was pretty low on my personal alert system. Besides, nobody was quite as good at ignoring red flags as I was. I was more comfortable than normal because it felt like my age and experience gave me an edge on him. Even if Matt wasn't the brightest or most mature bulb in the lamp, he seemed sweet and potentially a lot of fun.

I had never dated someone younger than me, but I had a girlfriend who had been in her mid-thirties when she married a man who was twenty-four. She was as happy as I wanted to be. It wasn't unthinkable. After all, those are just numbers; they have nothing to do with chemistry, right? Such are the things I tried to sell myself.

I thought, "Maybe a young guy is the answer after all I've gone through." I invited him to come spend a weekend with me.

Even before he arrived, I started picking up on small warning signs. There was the short attention span. Matt would be distracted by the TV while we were Facetiming, and our video calls got briefer and briefer. This guy was never going to be saddled with the label "fascinating conversationalist." I took a breath and decided to let it play out. If it was nothing more than a fun time for a short while, I was okay with that. At least that's what I told myself. I knew Jessica Wilde would have run with it and left the worry to the worriers.

The weekend turned out just about perfect, especially for an introvert like me. Matt was easy to be with and nobody was trying to impress anyone. We just hung out in my condo. Except for a little local bar hopping, we spent most of the time on my couch. We ordered pizza and scoped out his UFC competition, pausing the video periodically for steamy make-out sessions. Saturday night, we moved the action into my bedroom and he discovered where I kept my heart. By the time he left on Sunday night, I knew I was good and properly sunk. I really liked this kid. So much for keeping it fun, casual, and disposable. We kept up our routine of video chats and agreed that I would visit him over New Year's. I wasn't going to stay at his parents' house, so he rented us an Airbnb. New romance is heady. A new year, a new guy, a fun city. What could go wrong?

I didn't have to wait long to find out. Out of the blue, he stopped liking or commenting on any of my Instagram posts. I checked his page and found that he had moved on. He was regularly following other women and liking their photos. This was yet another part of the social media trap, part of the digital dark corners. It's so easy to stitch together a crazy narrative with this type of paltry information. It's like a bad detective story where one faulty clue is paired with another until a blurry picture reveals itself. On social media, that picture was usually false. I knew that. Still, what little I was seeing wasn't pretty.

By the time he picked me up at Calgary International Airport arrivals I had doubts and excitement in equal measure. We drove through Calgary to the place he had rented. I was disappointed to discover he had cheaped out. The ratty apartment was a poorly kept, dirty dive in the middle of a dicey section of downtown Calgary. I gave him the benefit of the doubt, assuming it was simple inexperience. He was young, after all, and could be excused for not putting together the pieces to understand a woman who owned her own condo didn't want to stay in a place with sticky counters and a bad roach problem.

We ordered Chinese takeout and settled in to watch TV. We had two days to kill before New Year's Eve. Matt invited me to dinner at his parents' house. It was going to be a big affair. The insecurities and doubts that had been growing were effectively stomped on; if he was introducing me to the family—to his parents—he had to be serious, right?

His family was the family I had always dreamed of: warm, welcoming, funny, and full of love. They embraced me wholeheartedly. His mother was generous and authentic with her hugs and his dad never let my wine glass go empty. It was a stark contrast to how Matt himself was treating me. He busied himself shotgunning beers with his brother-in-law down in the basement. Then he spent the rest of the night chasing the little kids in the family around the rumpus room while I hung out talking to the adult relatives upstairs. It was a strange experience.

We had tickets to see the Calgary Flames play the Edmonton Oilers on New Year's Eve. We were going to the game with a rowdy group of Matt's friends. I was pumped to get to know his buddies and I wanted to make a good impression. I painted on my tightest black mini dress and spent way too much time on my hair and makeup.

The night began full of promise. His pals' girlfriends welcomed me into their tightknit group with open arms. Matt's buddies were all fun-loving types, the kind of down-to-earth regular Joes that I had gone to school with. The Grey Goose flowed, everyone chatted, and the action on the ice rink was fast-paced. There was that electric feeling, the buzz when everyone in a group seems to tacitly agree that it will be a fantastically festive, memorable night.

The only person not on that page was Matt. He indulged in a deep and obvious sulk and it was left to me to puzzle out what the hell was causing it. He spent the better part of a fun night ignoring me. I had to congratulate myself on knowing how to pick them. Again.

As the third period came to a close, I decided to be the cool new girlfriend and pick up the bar tab. We gathered our stuff and headed for the exit. As we merged with the crowd, a guy turned to me and said, "Are you Jessica Wilde?" This is an irritation for a lot of big-name celebrities who come to value nothing quite so much as privacy. But for someone like me, a validation addict, it's a fix. I flat-out loved that kind of attention.

"Yes, hi!"

"Wow, I love your pics."

"Thanks, that means a lot."

I thought it might impress Matt that his girlfriend was a recognizable celebrity. He was sleeping with a star! Instead, he pulled a long face like he had just stepped in something warm, smelly, and squishy. He made a beeline for the exit, leaving me in the dust. I couldn't understand it. All this nonsense had killed a night that should have been pure, unbridled fun. The chilly Calgary air was an invitation to huddle in a bar, laugh, and drink to a new year and new prospects. We were surrounded by his good-natured friends who were ready to close out a wonderful New Year's Eve. Matt wasn't in the mood. He hustled us back to the grotty rental and treated me to the silent treatment until I finally fell asleep ten minutes after midnight.

The next morning, he was as cheery as if the night before hadn't happened. Or maybe we had experienced two different nights. Me? I went along. I avoided the big issue and the hard talk we should have had. That's what I had learned to do with my mother, and it's what I had done in all my relationships.

Looking back, I so clearly should have called him out on his bullshit. I didn't want to rock the boat, though. I didn't want to get to that end point that smacked of abandonment, even if I clearly knew that I was nowhere close to being in love with this guy. I had been down this road far enough to know that this wasn't how healthy relationships were built. At least my head knew that.

I kept my thoughts to myself and we spent my last two days in Calgary camping in the lumpy rental bed, eating unhealthy takeout food, and watching bad TV. That all served to calm my natural insecurities.

By the time I packed up and headed to the airport, I started thinking that maybe I was dramatizing everything. Maybe I was reading way too much into how he had ignored me around his family and friends. Maybe that was what young guys always did. Waiting for my flight, I took a huge leap of faith. I pulled out my iPhone and posted a photo of the two of us on my Instagram page.

I spent the next two days carefully checking the comments to delete anything negative before Matt could read it. I was pleasantly surprised when he reposted the photo on his own Instagram page. The comments flew in from his friends. Far more than for any other image he had ever posted. They were uniformly positive, with friends, family, and followers all congratulating him on landing me as a girlfriend. Subtext: He was a lucky, lucky guy. I should have been savvy enough to calculate how that would sit with an immature alpha-male personality.

This is one of the sneaky aspects of Instagram. A bunch of comments on one picture from a herd of followers I didn't even know, and my head inflated. That fucking delicious jolt of validation, the fix that hooked so many people. It wasn't working quite the same magic on young Matt. Turns out, he did not appreciate playing what he saw as second fiddle to a woman. MMA fighters are nothing if not insecure, testosterone-fueled, hyper-competitive egos.

A few hours after he posted the picture, I got a text: "Sorry, I can't do this anymore."

I had a completely new experience staring at that text. There wasn't the devastation of happiness having slipped away. Instead, a new thought popped into my head.

"You're dumping me? You? The guy that lives with his parents and still shotguns beers?"

It was a relief not to feel the stab of abandonment. I didn't miss Matt.

However, I wasn't totally in the clear, either. Some of those old feelings persisted. Here I was again, sitting alone in my condo, going down that familiar path of wondering what the hell was wrong with me. What was so flawed with me that even this dumbass kid couldn't fall in love with who I was? I had a bank vault of love, a mountain of heartfelt affection to offer. I wanted to give it. I wanted to love, and I wanted to be loved. I had my shit together, mostly. I made a good living. I felt like I was a better mom than my mother had been. I was a caring person who could pay attention to someone else's needs. I brought something valuable to the party. I knew I did.

My dog understood all that, but here I was, tossed aside by some stupid kid. I spent a couple of days asking myself questions to which I knew there were no satisfying answers. Fortunately, he wasn't much of a loss, so it hurt a lot less than losing Tyler or Moe had.

I thought again and again about the role Instagram had played in the whole messy drama. How stupid and destructive. Oddly, at the end of it all duty called. I still had to feed that social media beast. I had a living to make and a future to blaze. I wasn't going to do that by nitpicking the many faults of the golden goose. The tool I used most was Instagram, but I also understood that it was time to stand on my own two feet, appreciate my own value, and stop being lured by the false high of Insta-validation.

# -9-

# WHO THE HELL DO I THINK I AM?

I might have had some big bones to pick with Instagram's identity warping, but I couldn't argue with the professional opportunities that site opened up for me. Influencers like me aren't looking to rake in direct ad revenue on the site because that's not how Instagram works. Regardless, there is a huge upside in promotional value because brands are always hunting for hot commodities, follower-magnets who can open the door to new audiences. As my numbers climbed, I landed on the radar of several companies. Edgy jewelry and apparel companies and other hip brands started to reach out to me to promote them.

I had been open on all my social media pages about my decade-long struggle to quit smoking. My latest tool in that ongoing battle was vaping. My favorite brand was blu. After posting a couple photos of Jessica Wilde sexily drawing on a blu vaping pen, a marketing manager from the company messaged me. They had a new promotional campaign called "Pledge" in the works. Would I be interested in participating? With visions of free lifetime vaping cartridges filling my head, I sent him my phone number and we scheduled a call.

"We're recruiting high-profile personalities to take a pledge of overcoming a lifelong fear, then we film them in the process of dealing head-on with that fear. Does that sound like something you'd want to jump into?"

"Yeah, that might be cool. What would you need me to do?"

"I can send along the offer package. Everything's laid out in there, but basically you identify a big fear. Something you've been scared of forever. Then we set up the situation for you to face that fear, and we film the whole thing. The clips will run on YouTube, Instagram. All across the board."

"Yeah, I'd love to do that. Shoot me the offer and details."

The offer was a whole lot of money. They weren't after Samantha or Tiffany. They wanted Jessica Wilde to promote blu, conquering her fear in the sexiest way possible. Problem was, Jessica didn't fear shit. I had no real fears either, except dying alone. I didn't see blu's marketing masterminds making hay with that one.

There it was, a little Madison Avenue paradox. If I wanted that payday I had to give Jessica a big, well-known, tangible fear. Something they could film, and that people could relate to. I had given Jessica big, perfect boobs, a saucy attitude, a Star Wars-themed leg tat, and a world all her own. So what the heck? I threw a rabid fear of heights into the mix.

Like any good Instagram influencer, I couldn't let reality get in the way of a good post and a big payday. I told the company that I couldn't make it halfway up a stepladder without freaking. They responded with my fear-facing epic test—a trip to Lake

Garda in Italy, to climb one of the steep, low-lying mountains that surrounded the resort destination's picturesque lake.

Deception. It seemed so natural for Jessica. Really, though? It wasn't just me. Deception is the currency of Instagram. And Facebook, Twitter, every dating site known to man, and even LinkedIn. Heck, it extends far beyond the dark digital realm; producers script the hell out of "reality" TV, creating carefully mapped-out plots with big reveals timed conveniently for sweeps week. It's all a tangle of manipulated images and messages. Reality TV stars make sure the highest bidder's products make it on camera, often without even using those products.

I, on the other hand, believed in blu. I used and enjoyed the company's vape pen and cartridges. I couldn't see how the promotional power of a made-up pledge was any less valid than just going on camera and saying the truth: I was a huge fan of the company and what they made. I wasn't just blowing smoke after all.

Lake Garda is nestled in the most beautiful part of Northern Italy. If you drew an east-west line connecting Milan and Venice, Lake Garda would be the center point. I was excited for my first trip to Italy. It seemed so much more exotic than England or Holland. A new European adventure. Broaden your horizons they call it. I called it getting the hell out of Dodge so that I could clear my head. As I always did, I expected far too much from the trip. Every new place I've ever gone, whether it's L.A., London, or Amsterdam, looms large as an opportunity to reinvent myself. I anticipate that moment I walk out of the airport and smell different air, see different people, and feel a different sun on my skin. No matter how many times I've been disappointed, I still can't take a long plane flight without expecting magic on the other end. I'm certain that when I get there, I'll be someone else. I'll step into a new and improved identity as I slide the card key through the reader on my hotel room door.

I am forever let down. Every single place I go, I find the "same old me." Same insecurities. Same self-critique. Same Jessica staring back at me in the mirror. Insane as it may seem, that has never stopped me from expecting the next trip to be different. Every new destination is a new, fresh chance for transformation. Every plane is taking me to an undiscovered utopia where reality is so much better. Until it's just another city.

I'm not even sure what I'm hoping to change. You grow through travel, but it's not the places themselves that change you. It's how you see them and how you view your own world. What I would only process and really take on board much later was that wherever you go, you drag yourself with you. That includes your history and problems and baggage and fears and so much more. You're just putting the same closet contents in a different closet.

Though it might not have been my personal time capsule of transformation, Lake Garda was easily one of the most beautiful places I'd ever seen. The pristine lake lies in a bowl formed by spiky mountains. The town and forested foothills are dotted with ancient fortresses. There is a grotto that dates from Caesar's Rome, and a lively downtown full of excellent trattorias, fun, informal bars, and touristy shops.

It is a holiday destination for many Europeans, and rightfully so. The town has a wonderfully old-world charm, but with the amenities you'd find in any modern European capital. The lake is stunning. No matter the vantage point, it's like staring at a postcard brought to life.

Right after I got settled in my hotel room, I met the film crew who was there to capture me conquering my fear of heights. There were five of them, all from England. They were good-natured, witty, and proved to be fun to hang out with over the three-day shoot. We had breakfast together every morning, and then they'd head out to set up. We'd film in the afternoon, getting the light and the action they wanted to capture.

Unfortunately, for someone who makes her living off an illusion, I'm not so good at creating one on camera. The crew had to have realized, as they filmed me climbing the steep, rope-lined trail to the top of one of Lake Garda's mountains, that I wasn't actually scared. After all, they had me do take after take. The director would send me back down the same trail, and tell me to come up "looking scared," or "like I've accomplished something big." They wanted me to act, plain and simple. They needed—as much as I did—to capture usable video.

I did my best, but I conclusively proved to myself that I'm no actress. I would feel utterly confident hosting a reality TV show, but I have zero true acting talent. I wrestled the entire time with that old nemesis, the Imposter Syndrome. I mostly felt plain stupid as the cameras rolled. How in the world did I get Jessica Wilde into all these situations? When I finally saw the clips from that campaign, I cringed and suffered a bout of secondhand embarrassment. Thankfully, blu was happy with the scenes we had filmed, and ran the video as part of their Pledge campaign. One more Instagram success under Jessica's belt.

A big upside to that shoot was that it got my creative juices flowing. By the time my plane landed in Kelowna, I had decided to put together a seventies-themed photoshoot.

A secret about me: I was born a decade or two too late. I am an unabashed lover of everything seventies. The fashion and fads from that decade have always made me swoon. I mean, feathered hair? Sign me up. Platform shoes and super bells? Let's go big and wide. *That 70s Show* was some of my favorite TV. I wanted the photoshoot to pay respectfully cheesy homage to the era that gave us Farrah Fawcett-Majors and *Wonder Woman*. Wallabees and clackers. Puka shell necklaces and Disco.

I knew that if I did it right, I'd have a motherlode of dynamite original images I could plaster on Instagram and maybe even some usable video to feed my YouTube channel. I pulled together a team of local talent who all agreed to do it for portfolio pieces. I even roped in a videographer to chronicle the shoot. As it came together, I was increasingly jazzed at what I saw would be a fun camera session. I convinced the owners of Skinny Duke's Glorious Emporium, a retro bar and restaurant that had just opened up in Kelowna, to let us use the space for an afternoon.

The photos we got from the shoot would be good fuel for the Jessica Wilde social media business, but they would only hold me for so long. New content is always king on a site like Instagram.

I was working hard and making progress, but it's easy to burn out in the social media game. You push, and push, and push. The pure hours that can go into a successful Instagram, Twitter, or Facebook account can grind you down. It's important to stay fresh. You don't want to recycle photos or posts; the audience always wants something new. At a point, I realized I needed a break and some time away to take stock and recharge my batteries. I decided that a vacation was in order, and I wanted to go somewhere out of my comfort zone. That place was Thailand (not coincidentally, it would be the perfect locale to capture a few drop-dead selfies to nourish the Instagram machine).

Bobby agreed to take Izzy and Sophie for three weeks, and I bought my tickets. I had expected to land in a sticky, hot, country where I'd be constantly uncomfortable and have difficulties being understood. I was way off base as it turned out.

Thailand was a paradise, a place you could lose yourself in your own senses. That was especially true in the huge coastal city of Phuket. It was exotic and lush, full of energy.

I had booked a room in the Wyndham Grand Phuket, the nicest hotel in the city. It had a spectacular view of the jungles outside the city, and came with its own infinity pool. I could hear jungle birds calling and far-off ebb and flow of the ocean. I was stunned by the sheer beauty, by the feel of the humidity on my skin, and the cool luxury of the marble floors that stretched out past the glass doors of my bedroom. I settled in, stripped off my clothes, and washed the flight off with a skinny dip in the pool. As I wrapped myself in the hotel-issue plush bathrobe and listened to the sounds of my first tropical night settle around me, I realized the vacation was just what the doctor ordered.

I pondered how far I had come. How could have the hotel maid or cashier I had been ever imagined this? It was amazing to think that the girl who had once been a frightened, battered ball of a human being curled into the smallest possible space on the late-night bus rolling slowly back to Kelowna and homelessness, was now standing and staring into a sunset made of dreams as it faded to black over a tropical jungle. It made me so appreciate that moment, that particular circumstance and instant, as the jewel of time it was.

I had finally learned that a new place, a foreign destination was never going to magically answer life's puzzles. A different location wasn't about the new me, and the new reality. I accepted Thailand as simply a beautiful getaway, and appreciated it for its exotic allure. I didn't need to hunt for a grand change anymore; I just wanted rest, relaxation, and a new perspective. Thailand offered all that. From elephant sanctuaries, to the photo-perfect beaches, to the Phuket Town weekend market, the island treated me to mind-clearing adventures and breathtaking beauty.

The vacation gave me a lot of time to think, and so did the long flight back home. Halfway to Canada I decided it was time for a self-edit. I was going to get a butt lift and a full leg tattoo. Plastic surgery was always a reliable way to recharge my self-esteem. It was how I bricked over Tiffany and built Jessica in her place. Much as that might have been a superficial solution to deeper issues, I've never had a problem with that.

I enjoy creating a new me and don't see anything inherently wrong with changing my appearance surgically. Look, I'm not critiquing anyone else, or suggesting they get modified. This is about me. My body, my choices. I got my first plastic surgery at twenty-one, buying a pair of perfect—if too-large—boobs. From that point on, I was hooked. It was a revelation; this imperfect girl inside me could look at a menu and change anything she might be insecure about. Where did I sign up?

Cosmetic changes make me feel better, but they are also cash in the bank. You want to make a million bucks as a social media influencer? You have to keep your money maker looking like a million bucks. That is the price of admission.

Twenty years ago, nobody talked about it. If it was obvious that someone in the public eye had gone out and had work done, it was whispered about—or ridiculed if they were open about it, like Joan Rivers was. It was as if anyone who had cosmetic surgery had crossed a line. Joe or Jane Average wasn't even aware of the vast options awaiting him or her in that great cosmetic alterations universe.

These days, though, everybody knows. Botox ads are plastered on buses and subways, and you can get a wrinkle-flattening treatment on your lunch break. You can literally Photoshop yourself in real life. Maybe you can't alter everything (isn't that where real Photoshop comes in?), but I find every little bit moves the needle. Especially when you're in the business of trying to portray perfection to millions of Internet strangers. I don't judge; and anyone who judges me can kiss my surgically enhanced money maker. If she's smart and independent, a girl's going to do what a girl's going to do.

There were two centers of the universe for the butt-tastic operation I was after: Los Angeles and Malaga, Spain. Given all the hassles I had encountered trying to get into the United States, and the fact that the two options cost roughly the same, I decided it was a good excuse to give Spain another try.

Malaga, Spain, is a drop-dead gorgeous stretch of real estate along the country's Costa del Sol. For those of us who didn't make it through high school Spanish, the name means "coast of the sun," and boy is it. Malaga is blasted with the kind of sunlight produced by Hollywood scrim lighting. Hills rise dramatically from a gorgeous coastline that runs south to Gibraltar, and even the modest houses in Malaga are to die for. You have to have money to call the place home. If there is a Spanish equivalent of Rodeo Drive, it runs through Malaga.

I checked into the recovery house where I would stay post-op. I had booked with Joanna, the woman who owned and ran the place. She was a kindhearted, raven-haired beauty in her mid-fifties. She spoke flawless English and was authentically caring.

Calling it a recovery house doesn't do the three-story structure justice. Marble floors, flower arrangements on every side table, bougainvillea covering the walls right outside my window, and tasteful art on all the walls. Chatting around a well-laid table that night with an international crowd of a dozen women recovering from their own surgeries, I was excited to be there and embarking on a new look.

The next morning, though, the nerves kicked in as soon as I woke up. I was about to go into surgery half a world away from Izzy, in a clinic where few people spoke English. Good grief, Jessica, what the hell were you thinking? This was par for my surgical course, part of my pre-op routine. I was always anxious and constantly second-guessed changes until they were done; then I was inevitably super happy with them.

Still, it was disconcerting. I'd never had surgery outside of Canada. I wasn't here for the fun and adventure. What if something went horribly wrong? What if I couldn't explain my pain or my problem? There was no chance to reach Izzy and I would never have put the burden of calming me down on her anyway. I didn't have any friends that I would feel comfortable calling other than Moe, and I didn't want to bother him.

As my taxi arrived to take me to the surgery center, I took one last look in the mirror. Time to suck it up, Buttercup.

I was the first patient of the day. The doctor was an affable guy in his mid-forties, balding, with thick glasses. He exuded confidence, as if he was giving me a flu shot instead of slicing up my butt in six different directions. I had picked him because he was world-renowned for what he was about to do to me. He marked up my backside for the cuts he would be making, all the while making jokes and small talk. The surgery was obviously going to be a walk in the park for this guy, but I simply could not stop worrying.

I woke up in no pain, but nauseous from the epidural I'd been given. For the next twenty-four hours, I was either sleeping or throwing up. By the time they moved me back to the recovery house, I was glad to be out of the hospital. I could barely walk, and the doctor had saddled me with a laundry list of medications to take—all the prescriptions in Spanish. Thank god for Joanna. She was a saint, waiting on me hand and foot and making sure I was fed, had the right meds at the right time, and didn't throw myself off the balcony of my third-floor room.

I was an unqualified mess. It was the roughest recovery I'd

ever dealt with. The only way I could avoid the pain was by lying on my stomach. I couldn't sit, couldn't lay on my back, and could barely walk. I missed Izzy more than I've ever missed anyone in my life. I missed Sophie almost as much. Joanna's house was a beautiful, comfortable sanctuary, but I missed my condo and my bed. I cried myself to sleep, night after night. I don't like pain pills and avoid them at all costs, but the pain was wearing me out. I'd jolt awake in a panic, not quite sure where I was. Without Joanna, I would have been utterly lost.

She was caring and generous with her time. Even though she had a dozen patients to look after, she would indulge me in long talk after long talk. Her simple, genuine kindness gave me strength. More than that, she was a font of wisdom.

I didn't realize at the time that I was learning from an older woman who had figured out many of life's riddles, including many of the puzzles that still plagued me. Joanna was an expert listener, but she was also completely open with me about her own experiences. She had once been married to a preening narcissist. She had divorced him and built her own business. She relied on no man to help her and was pure confidence in motion. She gently laid bare things I needed to look at within myself. She offered a real-world example of how to conduct myself, how I could go forward. The fact that she had gone through what she had, that she was now successful and happy through her own efforts and inner strength, convinced me that I was strong enough to go it alone myself.

She was the mother I so wished I had. It dawned on me that under her wing, perhaps I was recovering from much, much more than just surgery.

Two weeks and one long, uncomfortable plane ride later, I walked through the door to my apartment to stacks of mail and the pure joy of my own space. Izzy and Sophie were already there; Bobby had dropped them off twenty minutes before I got home. It was heaven to see those two, to hug my daughter as if I would never let her go. I drank in her smile and fired question after question at her. There could not have been a better sound, better medicine, than her laugh. She made jokes about my butt, rolled her eyes in her own Izzy way, and we both teased Sophie who had apparently decided that as long as she attached her hip to my ankle, I couldn't possibly disappear for another three weeks. It was indescribably good to be home with those two.

Joanna had sent me home with a present: renewed inner strength. I stood on my own two legs—if kind of shaky courtesy of a sore, healing butt—confident in my own strength, abilities, and independence.


Ah, it would be lovely if it were all so easy as a single light bulb moment, the satisfaction of a life-changing epiphany. Come to a conclusion, settle in, be happy. Life, however, does not work that way. We rarely evolve and grow by leaps and bounds. It happens mostly by degrees. We learn in fits and starts, prisoners of mazes that are our own patterns. I still find myself sitting over a mug of morning coffee checking out guys on Instagram. I'm drawn to the same carefully managed, edgy handsomeness, the same cockiness and telltale signs of an emotionally distant asshole. These days, though, I don't pull the trigger. I don't swipe right. I don't get close enough to get burned. Progress. Sure, it's baby steps, but progress.

I spend more time on what I do have, than on what I don't. Izzy is the jewel in the crown of my life. She is my happiness. On the flip side, I have managed to cut my mother enough slack so that she could float far away, even if I never truly cut her loose. Her threat about a lawyer suing Bobby and me for "grandparent rights"? It never came to anything. How could it? I try to take all that has happened between her and I in stride. I realize now that I don't need to rise to the bait.

We still have lunch every couple of months. She talks about her life, and I let her. I want nothing to do with what I see as her dramas, so I keep it surface level. Some people you can safely hug; others you keep at arm's length. It's another thing I've made my peace with: I will never be able to talk to her about my childhood and my resentments.

We will never, ever have that frank talk that winds up in tears of regret, remorse, and a new start, our arms wrapped lovingly around each other. We can't. I suspect that our interactions will—in my view—always and forever be about her. I know now that even though I may be damaged—and certainly, I am—perhaps she is too. Perhaps I didn't give her space for having human flaws and failings. I think of her as the more wounded bird between us. I can afford to at least acknowledge that and show her a measure of compassion.

More and more, I extend that same compassion to myself. I don't beat myself up when I lay in bed on a Friday night far too early for a gal in her mid-thirties to be in bed. I don't criticize myself as I prop up my pillows, lean back, and scan interesting

Instagram pages to see what other influencers are doing. Sophie snuggles in next to me. Soon enough, she begins snoring as loud as an idling tractor. I browse and I think, and once in a while I come across some hunk's Instagram page and stop. I'll look through his pictures and wonder what he's really like. What is the truth behind him? One thing's for sure—he's nothing like that polished Instagram man-marvel. I put my phone on the nightstand, turn out the light, and count my blessings.

Truth be told, I'm human. I'm still capable of beating myself up once in a while. Every so often I make the mistake of going down my dark, familiar path of wondering what the hell is wrong with me.

Love seems so basic and yet so elusive. People do figure it out, I know they do. It's like a secret only some have been told. I feel this even though I know Instagram continues to be a wall between me and any relationship.

I wrestle with the fact that there is clearly no real value in social media. I've been to Oz and pulled back the curtain. I can't deny the gross manipulation involved in creating and refining an online identity. I see my competitors, all these beautiful young women, and often wonder what sets me apart from them? I don't know that anything does, to be honest.

I pop up on my followers' screens on nearly a daily basis. I'm literally in their faces. The image they see? It is what they want to believe it is—sultry dream girl, tattooed wild child, empowered woman not to be fucked with. They look and they look. But they don't see me. They don't see *me*.

I know that now. All too well. It's why I have to see myself, see the real image in the mirror. I focus on the caring mom I know

I am. I try not to dwell on the fact that the real me is alone when so many guys desire Instagram Jessica. Sure, I might spend a couple of days asking myself questions to which I know there are no satisfying answers. Camp out eating a banquet of junk food and feeling a little punk. Maybe once a year I fall down into the bulimia trap, but I jump right back out.

Those occasional dark moments are why these days I spend a good amount of time looking beyond the manufactured Jessica, to the future. I hope to nourish something healthier, a positive personality that will give me the voice to break out of the Instagram box. I want to challenge myself. I want to grow a career in entertainment. I want to make sure Izzy is happy in whatever she chooses for her own life. I want to figure out the riddle of romance and find the man who will embrace the not-Instagram me. The introvert who loves nothing more than a popcorn-munching Friday night on the couch spent watching a truly bad romcom. I want the guy who will sit next to me because he knows that's the real me and loves her.

I have figured this much out: Life is a love story, one way or another. Chasing it, giving it, aching for it. Check, check, and check. But love means so much more than just a significant other in your life. It's about acceptance, and caring, and respect. I've discovered all that starts with loving yourself, giving yourself room to be flawed, or sometimes, just be. I'm not talking about adulation or ego. I'm talking about extending the same compassion and tenderness toward yourself that you would to your child or a dear, dear friend.

Eventually, always, work beckons. Until I manage to build

that fortune big enough to retire, I have that endless wide maw of social media to face. I have to make a living. I can't do that by pining for a man I haven't met, nursing old wounds, or criticizing the golden goose. I trust that I'll eventually figure out how to move to the happy horizon. How to stand strong on my own two feet, understand my own value, and not be tricked by Insta-validation again.

For the moment, I've taken a break from the search for love. I need time off from anything with a penis. Joanna taught me something I should have realized so very long ago, something that should have been incredibly obvious. She helped me realize that I need to become better acquainted with the person I can really trust, someone who cares about me and someone I can count on. It's time to dig her out, and reacquaint myself with the real Jessica Wilde, the strong, if human, bitch underneath the Instagram photos.

We are all constantly making and remaking ourselves whether we know it or not. The reality is that we are not the Instagram illusions we present to the world online. Then again, we aren't the person our co-workers see, or the bartender thinks he knows. That's because we are works in progress, paintings never finished. We all use different brushes. Some people work in oils in dark, dramatic colors, others in pastel watercolors. I'm making my peace with the constant transformation. I have left behind the Tiffany and Samantha I once was, but the process of finding, defining, and refining the Jessica I am, goes on.

I can look at that babe on Instagram now, with her arched back and come-fuck-me stare. I know her. We share DNA. I understand it now. I am all she is, but she is not all I am. She's like my favorite dress, or the perfect shade of lipstick. She's the window dressing. Me? I'm Jessica Wilde, the real woman. I'm Izzy's mom, Sophie's human, flawed and perfect, tough bitch and occasional weakling. I'm the hopeless romantic. Instagram influencer, former homeless teen, kettlebell badass, and Canadian patriot. Yeah, I'm Jessica Wilde. And I'm okay with that.

## ABOUT THE AUTHOR

Jessica Wilde is a writer, Instagram celebrity, and tattoo model based in Kelowna, British Columbia. Born in 1988 in Canada, she was given up for adoption at birth, married at nineteen, and a mother at twenty. To escape poverty, she began an online career as a "cam girl," eventually moving on to become a social media influencer and brand ambassador for *Inked* magazine, and several luxury goods companies. She has modelled extensively, appearing on the covers of every major tattoo magazine, and hosting *Inked* magazine's cover girl competition. She wrote the monthly advice column "Wilde About Sex," for five years. She lives with her daughter Izzy, and Staffordshire terrier, Sophie, and balances a love of junk food with an exhausting gym schedule. This is her first book.

Made in the USA
Las Vegas, NV
13 October 2021

32271154R00129